The Life of Monsieur de Molière

Molière (Jean-Baptiste Poquelin), 1622–1673
Portrait by Pierre Mignard

The Life of Monsieur de Molière

Mikhail Bulgakov

Translated by Mirra Ginsburg

A New Directions Book

Manufactured in the United States of America
Originally published by Funk & Wagnalls, Inc., in 1970
Reissued clothbound and as New Directions Paperbook 601 in 1986
Published simultaneously in Canada by Penguin Books Canada Limited

Library of Congress Cataloging-in-Publication Data

Bulgakov, Mikhail Afanas'evich, 1891-1940.
    The life of Monsieur de Molière.
    (A New Directions Book)
    Translation of: Zhizn' gospodina de Mol'era.
    Reprint. Originally published: New York : Funk &
Wagnalls, c1970.
    Bibliography: p. 249
    Includes index.
    1. Molière, 1622-1673—Biography.   2. Dramatists,
French—17th century—Biography.   I. Title.
PQ1852.B813   1986   842'.4   85-32001

ISBN 0-8112-0956-3 (pbk.)

New Directions Books are published for James Laughlin
by New Directions Publishing Corporation,
80 Eighth Avenue, New York 10011

SECOND PRINTING

Contents

CONTENTS

Translator's Preface

Mikhail Bulgakov's *The Life of Monsieur de Molière* is more than a biography. It is a book by one artist about another, with whom he feels a deep affinity. There is much besides their craft that links these two men across the centuries. Both had a sharp satirical eye and an infinite capacity for capturing the absurd and the comic, the mean and the grotesque; both had to live and write under autocracies; both were fearless and uncompromising in speaking of what they saw, evoking storms with each new work; and both shared what Bulgakov calls "the incurable disease of passion for the theater."

Bulgakov, playwright, novelist, and short story writer, was born in Kiev in 1891, the son of a professor of the Kiev Theological Academy. Graduated from medical school in 1916, he practiced medicine for a short time, then abandoned it for writing. In 1921 he went to Moscow, a city ravaged, cold, and starving after the upheavals of war and revolution, and immersed himself in its miraculously teeming literary life. For several years he worked as a reporter and contributor of short satirical pieces to newspapers and periodicals, writing his first major novel, *The White Guard,* at night. Only the first part of the novel appeared in 1925. Its characters were members of the Russian gentry intelligentsia. Because Bulgakov treated them with sympathy as human beings swamped by the cataclysms of the time, the novel provoked an outburst of abuse from Communist critics, who branded him a "neo-bourgeois," "an internal émigré," and "an apologist for the class enemy." Despite this, the Moscow Art Theatre invited him to dramatize the novel and produced the play in 1926, under the title of *The Days of the Turbins.* The success of the play was instant and enormous, but, like the novel, it was followed by a storm of violent criticism.

As in Molière's case, this set the pattern for Bulgakov's entire subsequent career. A series of brilliant works, success, and the inevitable storm of abuse; plays accepted for production, rehearsed, then banned at the last moment; occasional brief lifting of the bans and their reimposition; and a constant struggle to speak and to be heard. Ironically, the seventeenth century dealt with Molière far more kindly than our own dealt with Bulgakov. Molière was able to write and to produce his works despite the scandals they provoked, thanks to the benevolent patronage of his spoiled, capricious King. A great admirer of the theater, the King was undisturbed by the playwright's thrusts at groups that, for his own purposes, he desired to keep in check. Bulgakov had to cope with a totalitarian state and a totalitarian ideology that would not tolerate dissent or original vision.

By 1930 Bulgakov was completely barred from either publication or production. In despair, he sent a letter to the government, asking permission to go abroad. To him, he said, the ban on his writing was tantamount to a death sentence. However—he went on—if he were not allowed to leave, he begged to be given work in his other field, the theater, as a director, an actor, an extra, or even a stagehand. Bulgakov was assigned to the Moscow Art Theatre as an assistant director and literary consultant, and continued in this capacity for several years. He was also permitted to dramatize the works of other writers, among them Gogol's *Dead Souls* and Cervantes' *Don Quixote*. The latter, significantly, was the last of his works to be produced in his lifetime.

Commenting admiringly on Molière's courage and persistence after the banning of *Tartuffe,* Bulgakov writes: "And what did the author of the luckless play do? Did he burn it? Or hide it? No. As soon as he recovered from the Versailles scandal, the unrepentant playwright sat down to write the fourth and fifth acts."

Further, prophetically, he says: "Yes, the play was banned, but it was impossible to stop its distribution, and it began to spread throughout France in handwritten copies. Moreover, rumors about the play reached other European countries."

Like his hero, Bulgakov, barred from his public, had the strength and courage to go on writing, and he left a large body of work that first began to come to light decades after his death, some of it, indeed, in handwritten or typewritten copies.

A lifelong admirer of Molière, Bulgakov worked on a play about Molière from 1930 to 1936. The play was admitted to production and its premiere took place in February of 1936. After seven performances, successful, as usual, and attended, as usual, by a barrage of official criticism, the play was withdrawn from the repertory.

The biography, dated 1932–1933, was not published until 1962, thirty years after it was written and twenty-two years after its author's death. "Who can illumine the tortuous paths of a comedian's life?" Bulgakov asks in *The Life of Monsieur de Molière*. "Who will explain to me why a play that could not be performed in 1664 and 1667 could be performed in 1669?"

One of the principal themes of *The Life of Monsieur de Molière*—the relation of the artist to his art and to society, especially a repressive society—runs through much of Bulgakov's work. It is found in his novel *The Master and Margarita,* in his play on Pushkin's death, *The Last Days,* in his play on Molière, *The Cabal of the Hypocrites,* and in other works. Another concern that is often evident is anxiety over the fate of manuscripts, of works already created but kept from publication or production. In *The Master and Margarita* Bulgakov's Satan, Woland, says majestically: "Manuscripts don't burn." In *The Life of Monsieur de Molière* Bulgakov speaks of the disappearance of all of Molière's manuscripts and letters—"as though conjured away into thin air."

Written during an extremely difficult period in Bulgakov's life and without any immediate hope of publication, *The Life of Monsieur de Molière* is nevertheless a work of grace and warmth. Like Yevgeny Zamyatin—another of that infinitesimally small group of creative artists who retained their integrity in the face of all pressures to conform—Bulgakov was not only a master stylist, but also a master of many styles. With great subtlety and sensitivity his writing reflects the spirit, the color, the rhythm, the very tone of the time and the characters he writes about.

In *The Life of Monsieur de Molière* the point of view is modern, yet also intimately of the period, as though Bulgakov were equally at home in both centuries, as though he were indeed both in the Moscow of the 1930s and also wearing a long caftan and writing with a goose quill. He is bound by no conventions, formal or academic. His attentive presence is felt throughout. He steps as easily out of his time into Molière's as he does into the reader's company. With complete and charming spontaneity he addresses his characters, or his readers, and this spontaneity is so artful that barriers of time and distance disappear. Bulgakov simply walks by the reader's side, and his occasional comment, wry or ironic or affectionate, is as welcome as the voice of a good friend.

The author's extensive research, his striving for absolute authenticity of fact and detail, never weigh down the narrative. Molière's difficult and dedicated life is treated with the insight and imagination of a brilliant novelist and playwright. "The artist must love his subject," wrote Bulgakov. Because of this love, because of Bulgakov's art and warmth and great sympathy, Molière emerges before us as a living, struggling, and ultimately tragic presence. And his biography reads like an absorbing novel, illuminating both the subject and the author. How infinitely moving, then, are Bulgakov's closing lines in which, suffocating in the vast prison of the spirit that Russia had become, he takes leave of the neglected bronze figure of his hero, sitting over a dried-out fountain in Paris: "There he is! It is he, the King's comedian, with bronze bows on his shoes. And I, who am never to see him, send him my farewell greetings."

Prologue
My Conversation With a Midwife

What can prevent me from laughingly telling the truth?
—HORACE

Molière was a famous writer of French comedies during the reign of Louis XIVth.
—ANTIOCH KANTEMIR*

A certain midwife, who had learned her art at the Maternity House of Divine Charity in Paris under the tutelage of the famed Louise Bourgeois, attended the most charming Madame Poquelin, née Cressé, on January 13, 1622, at the birth of her first child, male, premature.

I can safely say that, were I able to explain to the estimable midwife just who it was that she was helping to bring into the world, she might have injured the infant, and hence France, in her flustered condition.

And now—I am dressed in a caftan with huge pockets, and in my hand I have a goose quill, not a steel pen. Wax candles burn before me, and my mind is inflamed.

---

* Antioch Kantemir (1708–1744) was an early Russian satirist and diplomat —Tr.

[1]

"Madame," I say, "be careful as you turn the infant, don't forget that it is premature. This infant's death would mean the gravest loss to your country!"

"Good God! Madame Poquelin will have another!"

"Madame Poquelin will never have another like him, nor will any other lady for several centuries to come."

"You amaze me, sir!"

"I am amazed myself. But you must realize that three centuries hence, in a distant country, I shall remember you only because you held the son of Monsieur Poquelin in your arms."

"I have held infants of much nobler birth in my arms."

"Ah, but what do you mean by 'noble'? This infant will become more famous than your reigning king, Louis XIII; he will become more famous than your next king, and that king, madame, will be called Louis the Great or the Sun King! My good lady, there is a distant land, unknown to you, which is called Muscovy. It is inhabited by people who speak a language strange to your ear. And before long the words of him you are helping into the world will reach this land. A certain Pole, the jester of Tsar Peter I, will translate them into the barbarian tongue, not from your language, but from the German.

"The jester, nicknamed the Samoyed King, will scribble clumsy lines with his scraping quill. Translator to the Russian Tsar, he will endeavor in his crude words to render in the tongue of Muscovy the lines of your infant's comedy *The Precious Ladies Ridiculed*.

"The *Roster of such comedies as are reposited in the Department of Ambassadors to Foreign Courts, as of this thirtieth day of May, of the year 1709*, names, among others,

[2]

the following: 'Clownade *About the Doctor Who Was Thrashed* (also known as *A Doctor Against His Will*),' and *'The Breed of Hercules, with Jupiter as the Chief Personage.'* We recognize them. The first is *The Doctor in Spite of Himself,* another comedy by your infant. The second is *Amphitryon,* also by him. The same *Amphitryon* which will be played by Monsieur de Molière and his comedians in Paris in 1668, in the presence of Pyotr Ivanov Potemkin, Ambassador from the court of Tsar Alexey Mikhailovich.

"And so you see that the Russians will learn in this very century about the man you are now helping into the world. O, link of ages! O, currents of enlightenment! This infant's words will be translated into German, into English, into Spanish and Dutch. Into Danish, Portuguese, Polish, Turkish, Russian. . . ."

"But is this possible, sir?"

"Don't interrupt me, madame! Into Greek! Into modern Greek, I mean. But also into ancient Greek. Into Hungarian, Rumanian, Czech, Swedish, Armenian, Arabic!"

"You astound me, sir!"

"Oh, that isn't all. I can name you dozens of writers translated into foreign languages who do not even deserve to be published in their own. But this one will not only be translated. He will himself become the subject of plays, and your own compatriots will compose dozens of them. Plays about him will also be written by Italians—among them Carlo Goldoni, who is said to have been born to the applause of the muses himself—and by Russians.

"And not only in your country, but also in others will writers imitate his plays and compose variations on them. Scholars in diverse lands will write detailed analyses of his

[3]

works, seeking step by step to reconstruct the mysterious thread of his life. They will prove to you that the man who is now showing but faint signs of life in your arms will influence many writers of future centuries, including my compatriots—unknown to you, but known to me—Griboyedov, Pushkin, and Gogol.

> You're right: that man will come through fire unharmed
> Who spends a single day with you,
> Who breathes the air you breathe
> And keeps his reason sound.
> Away from Moscow! Never to return.
> I flee without a backward glance, to travel the wide world
> And seek some quiet corner where an injured heart can rest!

"These lines are from the end of *Woe from Wit* by my compatriot Griboyedov.

"And now hear this:

> And I, weighed down by injustice and betrayed by all,
> Shall leave this pit where vice is king,
> And go to seek a corner in a distant land
> Where one is free to be an honorable man!

"These are lines from a play by this very Poquelin, *The Misanthrope,* to be translated one day, almost two hundred years from now, by the Russian writer Fyodor Kokoshkin.

"Is there a similarity between these endings? Ah, good God! I'm not an expert, let scholars look into the matter! They will tell you how closely Griboyedov's Chatsky resembles Alceste the Misanthrope, and why Carlo Goldoni is considered a pupil of your Poquelin, and how Pushkin as a youth had imitated this Poquelin, and many other clever and interesting facts. I myself know little about it.

"But I am concerned with something else: my hero's plays will be performed for three centuries on all the stages of the world, and no one can tell when people will stop performing them. This is what interests me! Such is the man this child will grow into!

"Oh, yes, I wanted to speak about the plays. A most estimable lady, Madame Aurore Dudevant, better known as George Sand, will be among those who shall write plays about my hero.

"In the finale of her play Molière will rise and say:

" 'I want to die at home. . . . I want to bless my daughter.'

"And Prince Condé, approaching him, will say:

" 'Lean on me, Molière!'

"And the actor du Parc, who, incidentally, will no longer be among the living at the time of Molière's death, will cry out, sobbing:

" 'O, to lose the only man I have ever loved!'

"Ladies are known to write with sentiment, there's not much to be done about it! But you, my poor and bloodied master! You did not want to die anywhere—either at home or away from home! And it is highly doubtful that, when the blood gushed from your mouth, you gave expression to a wish to bless your daughter Esprit-Madeleine, who is scarcely of any interest to anyone!

"Who writes more touchingly than ladies? Why, some men. The Russian author Vladimir Rafailovich Zotov will provide an equally soul-felt finale.

" 'The King is coming. He wishes to see Molière. Molière! What's happened to him?'

" 'He died.'

"And the Prince, running to meet Louis, will exclaim:

" 'Sire! Molière is dead!'

"And Louis XIV will remove his hat and say:

" 'Molière is deathless!'

"Who can gainsay these words? Yes, a man who has now lived more than three hundred years is surely deathless. But the question is whether the King had recognized it.

"In the opera *Arethuse*, composed by Monsieur Campra, it was proclaimed:

" 'Gods rule the heavens, and Louis rules the earth!'

"The one who ruled the earth had never removed his hat before anyone but ladies, and would not have come to visit the dying Molière. And indeed, he did not come, nor did the Prince. The one who ruled the earth regarded only himself as deathless, but I believe he was mistaken in this. He was mortal like everyone else, and hence, blind. Were he not blind, he might have come to the dying man, for he would have foreseen the remarkable things to happen in the future and would, perhaps, have wished to touch true immortality.

"He would have had a glimpse, in the Paris of my time, on the sharp corner where the streets of Richelieu, Thérèse, and Molière converge, of a man sitting motionless between the columns. Below the man—two women of light marble, with scrolls in their hands. And still lower—lions' heads over the dried-up basin of a fountain.

"There he is, the cunning and enchanting Gaul, the King's comedian and playwright! There he is, in a bronze peruke and with bronze bows on his shoes! There he is, the king of French drama!

[6]

"Ah, dear lady! Why do you talk to me about the high-born infants you have once held in your arms? You must realize that the child you are holding now in the Poquelin home is none other than Monsieur de Molière! Ah! I see you understood me. Be careful, then, I beg you! Tell me, did he cry out? Is he breathing? . . . He is alive!"

Chapter 1

In the Monkey House

And so, on about the thirteenth of January, 1622, the first child, a sickly infant, was born in Paris to Monsieur Jean-Baptiste Poquelin and his spouse, Marie Cressé Poquelin. On January 15 he was christened in the church of Saint Eustache and named, in honor of his father, Jean-Baptiste. Neighbors congratulated Poquelin, and it became known in the upholsterers' guild that yet another upholsterer and furniture merchant had come into the world.

Every architect follows his own fancy. At the corners of the pleasant three-story house with a pointed roof sloping down on either side, situated on the corner of rue Saint Honoré and rue des Vielles-Étuves, the street of the Old Baths, the fifteenth-century builder had placed wooden carvings of orange trees with neatly trimmed branches. Along these trees stretched a chain of tiny monkeys plucking the fruit. Naturally, the house became known among Parisians as the monkey house. And the comedian Molière had to pay dearly later on for these marmosets! Many a well-wisher was to say that it was no wonder the elder son of the estimable Poquelin had chosen the career of a buffoon. What, indeed, could be expected of a man who had grown up in the company of grimacing monkeys? Nevertheless, the future comedian never renounced his monkeys; and in his later days, designing his coat of arms—heaven alone knows what he needed it for—he depicted on it his long-tailed friends, the guardians of his childhood home.

This home was situated in the noisiest commercial section in the center of Paris, not far from Pont-Neuf. The house was owned by Jean-Baptiste the father, Upholsterer and Draper to the Royal Court, who both lived and conducted his business in it.

In time the upholsterer attained yet another title—that of Valet to His Majesty, the King of France. And he not only bore this title with honor, but also secured its succession for his elder son, Jean-Baptiste.

It was rumored on the quiet that Jean-Baptiste the father, in addition to selling armchairs and wallpaper, engaged in lending money at handsome interest. I see nothing prejudicial in that for a merchant. But evil tongues asserted that Poquelin the elder somewhat overdid it in regard to interest extracted, and that the playwright Molière depicted his own father in the image of the revolting miser Harpagon. And Harpagon was the man who tried to palm off on a client all sorts of rubbish in lieu of money, including a crocodile stuffed with hay, which, he suggested, could be suspended from the ceiling as a decoration.

I refuse to believe these empty gossip-mongers! The dramatist Molière did not malign his father's memory, and I will not malign it either.

Poquelin the father was a merchant, an eminent and respected member of his honorable guild. He sold his wares, and the entrance to the monkey shop was adorned with a flag bearing, yet once more, the image of the monkey.

The darkish first floor, taken up by the shop, smelled of paint and wool, coins tinkled in the cash box, and all day long a stream of customers arrived to choose rugs and wallpaper. Among the customers were both bourgeois and aristocrats. And in the back, in the workshop with windows looking out upon the courtyard, the air was dense with dust, chairs were piled on chairs, everything was littered with pieces of furniture wood, scraps of leather and fabric; and in the midst of this chaos Poquelin's master workmen and apprentices were busily at work with hammers and scissors.

The rooms on the second story, above the flag, were the mother's domain, filled with the sounds of her constant, light coughing and the rustle of her heavy skirts. Marie Poquelin was a woman of substance. Her chests were filled with expensive dresses, cuts of Florentine materials, underwear of the finest linen. In the drawers she kept necklaces, diamond bracelets, pearls, emerald rings, gold watches, and costly table silver. When she prayed, Marie fingered a rosary of mother of pearl. She read the Bible, and was even said —although I do not put much credence in it—to have read the Greek writer Plutarch in abridged translation. She was quiet, amiable, and educated. Most of her forebears had been upholsterers, but there had also been occasional men of other professions, such as musicians and lawyers.

There was also in the upstairs rooms of the monkey house a fair-haired, thick-lipped boy. He was the eldest son, Jean-Baptiste. Sometimes he came down to the shop and the workshops and interfered with the apprentices, plying them with endless questions. The master workmen laughed good-naturedly at his stuttering, but were fond of him. At times he sat by the window, resting his cheeks on his fists, and looked at the dirty street where people hurried to and fro.

On one occasion, his mother, passing by, patted him on the back and said:

"Ah, my contemplator . . ."

And one fine day the contemplator was sent off to the parish school. At the parish school he learned precisely what could be learned in such a school; namely, he mastered the first four rules of arithmetic, learned to read freely, assimilated the rudiments of Latin, and became acquainted with many interesting facts related in the *Lives of the Saints*.

And life went on, peacefully and happily. Poquelin the elder was growing wealthier, there were now four children, when suddenly misfortune struck the monkey house.

In the spring of 1632 the delicate mother took ill. Her eyes began to glitter and looked strangely troubled. Within a single month she became so thin that she was scarcely recognizable, and ominous red spots bloomed on her pale cheeks. Then she began to cough blood, and a succession of doctors, mounted on donkeys and wearing sinister tall caps, began to frequent the monkey house. On May 15 the plump contemplator sobbed loudly, wiping his tears with grimy fists, and the entire household sobbed with him. The quiet Marie Poquelin lay motionless, her arms crossed on her breast.

When she was buried, it was as though a constant twilight settled over the house. The father fell into a melancholy and an absent-mindedness, and his firstborn saw him several times sitting alone on dark summer evenings, crying. The contemplator would get upset and wander all over the house, not knowing how to occupy himself. But then the father stopped crying and began to frequent a certain family by the name of Fleurette, and the eleven-year-old Jean-Baptiste was told that he would have a new mother. Soon after that Catherine Fleurette, the new mother, appeared in the monkey house. At this point, however, the family left the monkey house, because the father had bought a new one.

Chapter 2

The Story of Two Theater Lovers

The new house was situated in the marketplace itself, in the district where the famous Saint Germain fair was usually held. And in the new place the enterprising Poquelin displayed his goods with even greater flair. In the old house Marie Cressé had governed the home and borne children; in the new one she was replaced by Catherine Fleurette. What can be said about this woman? Nothing, it seems to me, either bad or good. But because she had entered the family as a stepmother, many of those who were interested in my hero's life began to say that the younger Jean-Baptiste had been ill-treated by Catherine Fleurette, that she was a bad stepmother, and that it was she who had served as the model for Béline, the faithless wife, in Molière's comedy *The Imaginary Invalid*.

I believe all this to be untrue. There is no evidence that Catherine mistreated Jean-Baptiste, and none to prove that Béline was she. Catherine Fleurette was not a bad second wife, and she fulfilled her mission on earth: a year after the wedding, she bore Poquelin a daughter, Catherine, and two years later another, Marguerite.

And so Jean-Baptiste was a pupil at the parish school and finally graduated from it. Poquelin the elder decided that his son had broadened his horizon quite sufficiently and ordered him to start paying attention to the business of the store. Jean-Baptiste began to measure cloth, to use hammer and nails, and to banter with the apprentices. And in his free time he read the well-worn little book of Plutarch left from the days of Marie Cressé.

And now, in the light of my candles, I see a gentleman of bourgeois appearance on my threshold, in a modest but respectable caftan, in a peruke, and with a cane in his hands. He is very lively for his years, with bright, alert eyes and good manners. His name is Louis, his surname Cressé. He is the father of the late Marie, and hence the grandfather of the younger Jean-Baptiste.

By occupation Monsieur Cressé was also an upholsterer. But Cressé was not a Court Upholsterer; he was a private merchant and conducted his trade in the Saint Germain market. He lived in a suburb of Paris, where he owned an excellent house with a good deal of land. On Sundays the Poquelin family usually went to visit the grandfather, and the children retained happy memories of these visits.

Well, then, the old Cressé and the young Jean-Baptiste became great friends. What could have bound the old man and the youngster? Perhaps the devil himself? Yes, surely, that was his work! Their mutual devotion, however, did not go unobserved for very long by Poquelin the elder, and soon provoked his glum astonishment. It turned out that

[14]

both grandfather and grandson were passionately in love with the theater!

On the free evenings, when the grandfather came to Paris, the two upholsterers, old and young, would exchange mysterious glances, whisper something, and leave the house. It was easy to discover where they turned their steps. They usually proceeded to the rue Mauconseil, where the King's players were giving performances in the low-ceilinged and gloomy Hôtel de Bourgogne. The estimable grandfather Cressé had firm connections with the elders of a certain society whose members were bound by both religious and commercial ties. This society was called the Fraternity of the Lord's Passion, and possessed the privilege of presenting mystery plays in Paris. It was this Fraternity that had built the Hôtel de Bourgogne, but at the time when Jean-Baptiste was a boy it no longer presented the mysteries, but leased the Hôtel to various groups of actors.

And so grandfather Cressé would pay a visit to one of the elders of the Fraternity, and the estimable upholsterer and his grandson would be given free seats in one of the unoccupied loges.

The leading actor at the Hôtel de Bourgogne theater at that time was the famous Bellerose. The troupe presented tragedies, tragicomedies, pastorals, and farces, and the foremost playwright of the Hôtel was Jean de Rotrou, a great admirer of Spanish dramatic models. Grandfather Cressé derived the greatest pleasure from the acting of Bellerose, and the grandson applauded heartily together with his grandfather. The grandson, however, preferred the farces to the tragedies enacted by Bellerose. These crude and light

[15]

farces, borrowed for the most part from the Italians, had found in Paris most excellent performers, who freely juggled topical comments in their comic roles.

Yes, to the misfortune of Poquelin the elder, grandfather Cressé had shown the boy the way to the Hôtel de Bourgogne! And together with his grandfather when he was a boy, and with comrades when he had grown into a youth, Jean-Baptiste had managed to see a great many marvelous plays at the Hôtel.

The famed Gros-Guillaume, who appeared in the farces, struck the boy's imagination with his flat-topped red beret and white coat barely closing over his monstrous belly. Another celebrated figure, Gaultier-Gargouille, dressed in a black camisole with red sleeves, with huge spectacles on his nose and a walking stick, also had the Bourgogne audience in stitches. Jean-Baptiste was equally impressed by Turlupin, with his inexhaustible store of tricks, and Alizon in the roles of ridiculous old women.

In the course of several years an endless number of figures whirled past Jean-Baptiste's eyes as in a carousel—pedantic doctors, old misers, bragging and cowardly captains, masked or made up with flour and paint. To the wild laughter of the audience, frivolous wives deceived their grumbling, stupid husbands, and comic bawds chattered away like magpies. Cunning, lightfooted servants led aged Gorgibuses by the nose, old fogies were thrashed with sticks and stuffed into sacks. And the walls of the Hôtel de Bourgogne shook with the roaring laughter of Frenchmen.

Having seen everything that could be seen at the Hôtel de Bourgogne, the infatuated upholsterers would proceed to another large theater, the Theater on the Swamp—the

Hôtel du Marais. This playhouse was the home of tragedy, in which the famous actor Montdory excelled, and of high comedy, the best examples of which were composed for this theater by the most eminent dramatist of the time, Pierre Corneille.

It was as though the grandson of Louis Cressé was immersed in turn in different waters. At the Bourgogne, Bellerose, adorned in finery like a rooster, declaimed in sugary, tender tones. He rolled his eyes; then, fixing them at some invisible distant point, he would wave his hat in a graceful gesture and recite his monologues in a singsong, so that it was impossible to tell whether he was speaking or singing. And at the Marais, Montdory would shake the walls with his thunderous voice and gurgle, dying tragically.

The boy returned to his father's house with fevered, glittering eyes, and at night he dreamed of the buffoons— Alizon, Jacquemin Jadot, Philippin, and the famed Jodelet with his chalk-white face.

Alas! The Hôtel de Bourgogne and the Swamp did not exhaust all possibilities for those sick with the incurable disease of passion for the theater.

At the Pont-Neuf and in the market district trade proceeded at full swing. Paris grew fat with it and spread out, growing more and more beautiful, in all directions. In the shops and in the street before them life ran riot, dazzling the eye and setting up a ringing in the ears. And where the Saint Germain fair spread its tents, it was a veritable Babel. Din! Clatter! And the filth, the filth!

"My God, my God!" the crippled poet Scarron exclaimed about the fair. "The mountains of filth that can be raised all over by rear ends unfamiliar with underpants!"

[17]

All day long the crowds shuffle, walk, mill about! The townsmen and their pretty women! The barbers in their shops busily shave, soap chins, pull teeth. Riders rise above the dense mass of pedestrians. Doctors, as ponderous and self-important as crows, ride by on mules. Royal musketeers, with the golden arrows of their insignia emblazoned on their coats, sit lightly on their cantering mounts. Capital of the world, eat, drink, trade, grow! Hey you, rear ends unfamiliar with underpants, come here, to the New Bridge! Look, they are setting up tents and draping rugs over them. Who is this, shrilling like a pipe? A crier. "Do not delay, sirs, hurry, the show is just about to begin! Don't miss the chance! Here only, and nowhere else, can you see the marvelous marionettes of Monsieur Brioché! There they swing over the dais on their cords! See the sensational trained monkeys of Fagotin!"

In the various stalls by Pont-Neuf there are street doctors, pullers of teeth, corn surgeons, and quack apothecaries. They sell the people panaceas against every illness, and often, the better to draw attention to themselves, they enter into compacts with itinerant street actors, or even with actors playing in the theaters, and the latter give entire performances demonstrating the miraculous properties of the cure-alls.

There are solemn processions. Comedians, dressed up and adorned with dubious, rented finery, ride by on horses, shouting advertisements and calling the people. Street urchins follow them in flocks, whistling, diving in and out among the feet of the crowd, and increasing the general pandemonium.

Thunder, Pont-Neuf! Amid your din I hear the birthcries of French comedy, born of the charlatan father and the actress mother. It screams piercingly, and its coarse face is powdered with flour!

All of Paris is agog over the mysterious, astonishing Christoforo Cantugi, the purveyor of "orviétan," who has engaged an entire company and opened a series of shows in a booth. There, with the aid of a group of punchinellos, he has begun to sell his universal nostrum:

> Nowhere else, you may be sure,
> Will you find a better cure!
> Orviétan, orviétan!
> Come and buy orviétan!

Masked buffoons swear in voices gone hoarse with shouting that there is no sickness in the world that cannot be cured by magical orviétan. "It will save you from consumption, it will drive away the plague, any itch, and any ache!"

A musketeer rides past the booth. His thoroughbred stallion squints with a bloodshot eye, foam drips from his bit. Strangers to underpants bar his way, cling to the saddle. Voices howl from the orviétan booth:

> *Monsieur le capitaine,*
> Won't you buy some orviétan?

"A plague on you! Out of my way," cries the guardsman.

"Let me have some orviétan," says a certain Sganarelle, tempted by the extravagant promises. "How much is it?"

"Sir," replies the charlatan, "orviétan is priceless! I cannot take money from you, sir!"

"Oh, my good sir," answers Sganarelle, "I realize that all the gold in Paris will not pay for this little box. But I could not possibly accept it as a gift. Here is thirty sous, if you please, and kindly give me my change."

As dark blue evening settles over Paris, lights go on. In the showbooths tallow candles drip in smoky, cross-shaped sconces, torches with swirling tails shed flickering light.

Sganarelle hurries home, to the rue Saint Denis. He is pulled by his coattails in all directions, urged to buy antidotes for every poison on earth.

The bridge clamors with a thousand noises.

And making their way through this human mass are a venerable grandfather and his adolescent companion in a crimped collar. And no one knows, and the actors on the boards do not suspect who it is that is being jostled in the crowd before the charlatan's booth. Jodelet at the Hôtel de Bourgogne does not know that one day he will be a member of this youngster's company. Pierre Corneille does not know that in his declining years he will be happy when this boy accepts his play for production and pays him, a playwright gradually sinking into poverty, money for the play.

"Shouldn't we take a look at the next booth, too?" the grandson asks in civil, melting tones.

The grandfather vacillates—it's late. But he cannot resist: "Oh, well, let us step in."

In the next booth an actor does tricks with a hat: he whirls it, folds it up into unusual shapes, crumples it, throws it up into the air . . .

And now the bridge is all lit up, and lanterns float throughout the city in the hands of pedestrians, and the piercing cry, "Orviétan," still lingers in the ears.

And it is very possible that in the evening the rue Saint

Denis witnesses the finale of one of Molière's future comedies. While Sganarelle or Gorgibus was buying orviétan, with which he hoped to cure his daughter Lucinde of her love for Clèante or Clitandre, Lucinde had naturally run off with this Clitandre and married him!

Gorgibus raves! He was deceived! He was hoodwinked! He throws the damned orviétan in the face of his maid! He threatens!

But jolly fiddlers will appear, the servant Champagne will break into a dance, Sganarelle will make peace with the accomplished fact. And Molière will write a happy end to the evening, with lantern illumination.

And so, thunder, Pont-Neuf!

Chapter 3
Should the Grandfather Be Given Orviétan?

One evening Cressé and his grandson came home, excited and, as always, somewhat mysterious. Father Poquelin was resting in his armchair after a day's work. He asked where the grandfather had taken his favorite. And, of course, they had been at the Hôtel de Bourgogne to see a play.

"What's all this running to the theater?" asked Poquelin. "Are you planning to turn the boy into a comedian?"

The grandfather put down his hat, deposited his cane in the corner, was silent a while, and then said:

"I wish to God he could become as fine an actor as Bellerose."

The Court Upholsterer's jaw dropped. After a silence, he inquired whether the old man was serious. But since Grandfather Cressé was silent, Poquelin himself went on to enlarge on the theme in ironic tones.

If, in the view of Louis Cressé, one could aspire to become like the comedian Bellerose, why not go further? Why not follow in the steps of Alizon, who clowned and capered on the stage, imitating old market women for the amuse-

[22]

ment of the townsmen? Why not smear one's face with some white trash and glue on a monstrous moustache, like Jodelet?

And, generally, why not play the fool instead of attending to business? After all, the Parisians paid for this at the rate of fifteen sous per person!

An excellent career, indeed, for the son of the Court Upholsterer, who is known, thank God, to all of Paris! Wouldn't the neighbors gloat to see the younger Monsieur Poquelin, who was to inherit the title of Royal Valet, on the stage! Everybody in the upholsterers' guild would split his sides with laughter!

"Forgive me," said Cressé mildly. "Do you mean to say that theater should not exist?"

But Poquelin denied any such meaning. There should be a theater. Even His Majesty, may the Lord prolong his days, recognizes the theater. The Bourgogne troupe was granted the title of Royal Company. All that was very well. He, Poquelin himself, was not averse to visiting the theater on a Sunday. But he would say that the theater existed for Jean-Baptiste Poquelin, and not vice versa.

Poquelin munched his toasted bread, washed it down with wine, and inveighed against the grandfather.

Yes, one might go even further. If one found no employment in His Majesty's troupe—and not everybody, good sirs, is a Bellerose, who is said to own twenty thousand livres' worth of costumes alone—then why not go and play at the fair? One could spout indecent jokes, make insinuating gestures, why not, why not? All the neighbors in the street would point their fingers!

[23]

"But pardon me, I am jesting," said Poquelin. "But then, of course, you were jesting too?"

But no one knows whether the grandfather was jesting, just as no one knows what the young Jean-Baptiste was thinking during his father's monologues.

"Queer people, those Cressés!" the Court Upholsterer thought to himself as he turned sleeplessly in his bed. "To say such things in the boy's presence! It would not have been proper, but the old man should really have been told that those were stupid jests!"

He could not sleep. The Court Upholsterer and Royal Valet stared into the dark. Ah, but all of those Cressés were alike! His first wife, may she rest in peace, was also full of fantasies and also adored the theater. But the old wretch was sixty! Honestly, it was ridiculous! He should be taking orviétan, he's falling into his second childhood!

All those worries. And the shop. Insomnia . . .

Chapter 4

Not Everybody Likes To Be
an Upholsterer

And yet, I feel sorry for poor Poquelin! Really, he seemed to be under a curse! In November of 1636 his second wife died too. Again he took to sitting in the dark with his misery. Now he would be altogether alone. And he had six children. And the shop was on his hands, and the upbringing of all the children. Alone, always alone. He could not marry a third time. . . .

And to add to it all, soon after the death of Catherine Fleurette something seemed to have come over his firstborn, Jean-Baptiste. The fourteen-year-old lad went into a strange decline. He was working in the shop; there could be no complaint against him, he did not idle away his time. But he moved, Heaven forgive me, like a marionette from Pont-Neuf. He lost weight; he took to sitting at the window and looking out, although there was nothing there, either new or interesting, to be seen; he lost his appetite. . . .

It was time to have a talk with him.

"What is it? Tell me what's wrong with you," asked the

father, adding in a strained voice, "You are not sick, I hope?"

Baptiste stared at his square-toed shoes and was silent.

"The troubles I have with you children," said the poor widower. "What shall I do with you all? Don't keep me worrying, tell me."

Baptiste raised his eyes to his father, then looked out of the window and said:

"I don't want to be an upholsterer."

Then he thought for a while, and evidently deciding to cut the knot at one stroke, he added:

"I feel a deep repugnance for it."

After another pause he added:

"I hate the shop."

And as a final blow at his father, he concluded:

"With all my heart and soul!"

After which he fell silent. And his face assumed a foolish expression. In fact, he did not know what would follow his announcement. Perhaps a slap in the face from his father. But there was no slap.

There was an interminable pause. What could be done in such an unheard-of situation? A slap? No, a slap would not solve anything. What could the father say to his son? That he was a fool? There he stood like a hitching post, and his face looked blank. But the eyes did not seem to be stupid, and they glittered like the eyes of Marie Cressé.

He doesn't like the shop? Perhaps he only imagines it? He is still a boy, at his age one cannot speak of what one likes or does not like. Perhaps he is simply a little tired? But he, the father, is still more tired, and he has no help from anyone, he has turned gray with cares. . . .

[26]

"But what do you want?" asked the father.

"To study," answered Baptiste.

At this moment someone knocked softly at the door with a cane, and Louis Cressé entered the room in the twilight.

"There," said the father, pointing at the fluted collar. "He does not wish to help me in the shop, you see, he wishes to study."

The grandfather began to speak in mild, conciliatory tones. Everything, he said, would turn out for the best. If the young man was unhappy, then, of course, it was necessary to do something about it.

"But what?" asked the father.

"Why not send him to school, for that matter?" exclaimed the grandfather.

"But he was graduated from the parish school!"

"Ah, what's the parish school!" said the grandfather. "A boy of his abilities . . ."

"Leave the room, Jean-Baptiste, I shall have a talk with your grandfather."

Jean-Baptiste went out. And a most serious conversation took place between Cressé and Poquelin.

I shall not repeat it to you. I shall merely exclaim: Oh, Louis Cressé of hallowed memory!

Chapter 5
For the Greater Glory
of God

The famous Collège de Clermont, later known as the Lycée
Louis-le-Grand, was indeed quite unlike the parish school.
The Collège was maintained by members of the powerful
Order of Jesus, and it must be admitted that the Jesuit
fathers did their job brilliantly—"for the greater glory of
God"—like everything else they put their hand to.

The Collège, headed by its Rector, Father Jacques Dinet,
was attended by nearly two thousand boys and youths of
noble and bourgeois families. Three hundred were resident
students, the rest lived at home. The Society of Jesus educated the flower of French youth.

The fathers taught courses in history, classical literature,
the juridical sciences, chemistry and physics, theology, philosophy, and Greek. As for Latin, that goes without saying.
The students at Clermont not only read and studied the
Latin authors constantly, but were required to converse in
Latin during recess hours between classes. You can easily
understand yourself that under such conditions it was not

[28]

difficult to assimilate this language so essential for human culture.

Special hours were devoted to dancing lessons. At other hours the halls resounded with the clanking of rapiers: French youths were learning to wield weapons so that they might defend the honor of the King of France in mass battle, and their own—in single combat. On gala occasions the resident students presented plays by ancient Roman authors, chiefly Publius Terentius and Seneca.

Such was the educational institution to which Louis Cressé had sent his grandson. Poquelin the father could by no means complain that his son, the future Royal Valet, was in bad company. The roster of Clermont students included the names of many highborn families; the highest nobility sent its sons to the Clermont lycée. At the time when Poquelin was attending the Collège, Clermont boasted of three princes among its students, one of whom was none other than Armand de Bourbon, Prince de Conti, the brother of another Bourbon, Louis Condé, duc d'Angoulême, later known as the Great. In other words, Poquelin was a fellow student of a personage of Royal blood. This alone would suffice to prove that the teaching at the Collège de Clermont was of a high level of excellence.

It must be noted, however, that the youths of blue blood were segregated from the sons of the wealthy bourgeois, of whom Jean-Baptiste was one. Princes and marquises were boarders at the lycée, with their own servants, their own instructors, their own separate hours of study, as well as their own separate classrooms.

It must further be said that Prince Conti, who will subsequently play an important role during the wanderings of my restless hero, was seven years younger than Jean-Baptiste. He was sent to Clermont as a young boy, and, naturally, never had any contact with our hero.

And so Poquelin the younger immersed himself in the study of Plautus, Terence, and Lucretius. According to custom, he let his hair grow down to his shoulders and wore out his wide trousers on the schoolbench, stuffing his head with Latin. The furniture shop was veiled in mist; he found himself in an altogether different world.

"It must be the will of fate," muttered Poquelin the elder, falling asleep. "Well, then, I shall have to turn the business over to the second son. And this one may, perhaps, become a lawyer, or a notary, or something along that line."

Did his boyhood passion for the theater die out in the heart of the scholar Baptiste? Alas, not in the least! Breaking out of the Latin vise during his free hours, he would still hurry off to Pont-Neuf and the theaters—this time not in his grandfather's company, but with several of his fellow students. And during his years at the Collège, Baptiste became thoroughly acquainted with the repertory of the Swamp and the Hôtel de Bourgogne. He saw Pierre Corneille's plays *The Widow, Place Royale, The Palace Gallery,* and the famous *The Cid,** which won its author wide renown and the envy of his fellow writers.

But this was not all. Toward the end of his days at the lycée, Jean-Baptiste had learned to find his way not only into the theater loges or pit, but also backstage, where he made one of the most important acquaintances of his life.

---

* All play titles mentioned in the text are given in French and English beginning on page 249.

[30]

He met a woman, Madeleine Béjart, an actress who played for a time in the Theater on the Swamp. Madeleine was a redhead, with exquisite manners and, by general consensus, a great and genuine talent. A fervent admirer of the dramatist Jean de Rotrou, Madeleine was intelligent, had fine taste, and, which was a great rarity, knew literature and herself wrote poetry. No wonder, then, that the enchanting Parisian actress completely captivated the Clermont student, who was four years her junior. What is interesting is that Madeleine reciprocated his feelings.

And so, the course of studies at the Collège lasted five years, and was crowned, so to speak, with the study of philosophy. And throughout those five years, Jean-Baptiste worked diligently, finding time, nevertheless, for visits to the theater.

Did my hero become an educated man at the Collège? I do not believe that any institution of learning can produce an educated man. But a well-conducted institution can turn out a disciplined man, with the habit of study that can later be of good use when the man begins to educate himself outside the walls of the school.

Yes, at the Collège de Clermont Jean-Baptiste was taught discipline; he was taught to respect knowledge and shown a way to it. When he was completing his course in 1639, his head was no longer filled with the odds and ends of his parish-school studies. His mind was laced, to quote Mephisto, in Spanish boots.

During his years at the lycée Poquelin struck up a friendship with a certain Claude-Emmanuel Chapelle, the illegitimate son of an eminent finance official, Pierre Luillier, a man of great wealth, whose home he began to visit. At the time when the young students were completing their studies, a remarkable man appeared at the Luillier home as a dear and welcome guest. The man's name was Pierre Gassendi.

Professor Gassendi, a native of Provence, was a highly educated man. His erudition could have been enough for ten men. He was a teacher of rhetoric, an excellent historian, a widely informed philosopher, physicist, and mathematician. The scope of his learning in the field of mathematics alone was so great that he was offered a chair at the Royal College. But mathematics did not exhaust Pierre Gassendi's intellectual baggage.

A keen and restless mind, he had begun his studies with the works of the most famous philosopher of antiquity, the peripatetic Aristotle, and, having studied him in the fullest measure, he came to detest him in the same measure. Then, after acquainting himself with the great heresy of the Pole Nicholas Copernicus, who had declared to the whole world that the ancients were mistaken in assuming that the earth was the motionless center of the universe, Pierre Gassendi became a fiery admirer of Copernicus.

Gassendi was enchanted with the great thinker Giordano Bruno, who had been burned at the stake in 1600 for insisting that the universe was infinite and contained a multitude of worlds.

Gassendi was heart and soul behind the brilliant physicist Galileo, who had been compelled with his hand on the Bible to renounce his conviction that the earth moved.

Anyone with courage enough to attack the teachings of Aristotle or the scholastic philosophers who followed him found a most loyal accomplice in Gassendi. He made a thorough study of the teachings of the Frenchman Pierre de la Ramée, who attacked Aristotle and perished during the Saint Bartholomew's Day massacre. He sympathized with the Spaniard Juan Luis Vives, who demolished scholastic philosophy, and the Englishman Francis Bacon, whose *Instauratio Magna* was written in opposition to Aristotle. But it is impossible to name them all!

Professor Gassendi was an innovator by nature; he admired clarity and simplicity of thought, had boundless faith in experience, and respected experimentation.

Beneath all this was the granite foundation of his own philosophy. This philosophy was derived from the same deep antiquity, from the philosopher Epicurus, who lived some three hundred years before our era.

If anyone had asked Epicurus for the formula of his teaching, he would probably have answered:

"What does every living creature strive for? Every living creature strives for pleasure. Why? Because pleasure is the highest good. Live wisely, then—and seek enduring pleasure."

The formula of Epicurus pleased Pierre Gassendi enormously, and in the course of time he constructed his own:

"The only thing man is born with," Gassendi would say to his pupils, tugging at his pointed scholarly beard, "is love for himself. And the goal of every man's life is happiness! But what elements does happiness consist of?" the philosopher would ask, his eyes flashing. "Only two, my friends, only two: a serene spirit and a healthy body. Any good doctor will tell you how to preserve your health. And I shall tell you how to achieve serenity of spirit: commit no crimes, my children, and you shall feel neither repentance nor regret, and only these make men unhappy."

[33]

MIKHAIL BULGAKOV

The Epicurean Gassendi began his scholarly career by producing a long work in which he argued the total worthlessness of Aristotelian astronomy and physics and defended the theory of Copernicus, of whom I spoke earlier. This most interesting work, however, remained unfinished. If anyone had asked the professor why this was so, I strongly suspect that he would have replied like a certain Chrysale, the hero of one of Molière's future comedies who said to an excessively learned lady, Philaminte:

> What, are our bodies trash?
> This trash to me is much too dear!

"I have no wish to go to prison, my dear sirs, because of Aristotle," Gassendi would have said.

And indeed, when this trash, your body, is thrown into prison, how, it may be asked, would your philosophic spirit fare?

In short, Gassendi stopped just in time; he did not complete his work on Aristotle and devoted himself to other pursuits. The Epicurean was too fond of life, and the edict passed by the Paris Parliament in 1624 was still too fresh. The point is that Aristotle was, if one may put it this way, canonized by all the learned faculties of the time, and the Parliamentary edict spoke quite unequivocally of the death penalty for all who dared to criticize Aristotle and his successors.

And so, having avoided serious unpleasantness, having journeyed through Belgium and Holland, and having written a number of significant works, Gassendi wound up in Paris, at the home of Luillier, his old friend.

Luillier was a clever man, and he asked the professor to

give private lessons to his son Chapelle. And since Luillier was not only clever but also generous, he permitted Chapelle to form a whole group of young men to share Gassendi's lectures with him.

This group included Chapelle, our Jean-Baptiste, a certain François Bernier, a young man with a passion for the natural sciences who later became a famous traveler in the Orient and was nicknamed "Great Mogol" by the Parisians, and finally, a personage entirely original and unlike the rest of the company. This last member was older than the others; he was not a student at Clermont, but a guards officer, recently wounded in battle, a drunkard, a duelist, a wit, a Don Juan, and a beginning playwright. While still in college in the city of Beauvais, in the class of rhetoric, he had composed an interesting drama, *The Tricked Pedant,* in which he satirized the director of his college, Jean Grangier. This guardsman's name was Cyrano de Bergerac.

And so this company, seated in Luillier's luxurious apartments, absorbed the fiery discourses of Pierre Gassendi. This was the man who polished my hero's mind! This Provençal with a face furrowed by passions! It was from him that Jean-Baptiste inherited the triumphant philosophy of Epicurus and a great deal of serious knowledge of the natural sciences. In the charming light of wax candles, Gassendi instilled in him a love for clear and precise thought and a hatred of scholasticism, respect for empirical experience and contempt for falseness and flowery bombast.

Then came the moment when both the Clermont Collège and Gassendi's lectures were over. My hero became an adult.

"You will now be kind enough to take a trip to Orléans," said Poquelin the elder to the graduate of Clermont, "and take an examination in jurisprudence. You must get a degree. And see that you don't fail, for I spent plenty of money on you."

And Jean-Baptiste went to Orléans to receive a diploma in jurisprudence. I do not know how much time he spent in Orléans, or the precise dates. But it seems to have taken place very early in 1641.

One of the innumerable slanderers who hated my hero asserted many years later that any ass could have received a learned degree in Orléans, provided he had money. This, however, is not true. An ass could not receive any degrees, nor did my hero resemble an ass in any way whatever.

True, some spirited young men who had gone to Orléans for their examinations related afterward that they had come to the university late in the evening and had roused the professors from sleep. They said further that the yawning professors had put on their scholarly hats over their greasy nightcaps, examined them then and there, and issued their degrees. But it may well be that these young men lied.

Whatever the situation in Orléans, it is definitely known that Jean-Baptiste won his degree as Licentiate in Law.

And so, the boy in his fluted collar and the long-haired scholar are no more. I see before me a young man in a light-colored wig.

I study this man avidly.

He is of medium height, slightly stooped, with a hollow chest. In the swarthy face with high cheekbones the eyes are wide-set, the chin sharp, and the nose wide and flat. In short, he is extremely unprepossessing. But his eyes are remarkable. I read in them a strange and everpresent caustic smile, and at the same time an unquenchable wonder at the surrounding world. There is something sensual, almost feminine in these eyes, but in reality there is a secret illness in their depths. Some worm, believe me, is already gnawing at this twenty-year-old man.

The man stutters and breathes improperly when he speaks. I can also see that he is quick-tempered and subject to abrupt changes of mood. He easily passes from moments of gaiety to moments of dark reflection. He finds ridiculous traits in men and likes to make them the butt of his jests.

On occasion he carelessly slips into frankness. At other times he tries to be secretive and cunning. He can be recklessly brave, but he can also shift within the moment to irresolution and cowardice. You must agree with me that with these characteristics he will not have an easy life, and will make many enemies!

But let him live his life!

Chapter 6

Improbable Adventures

The time we are describing was a stormy period for France. It had only seemed quiet at the Collège de Clermont or at the father's shop.

France was shaken by foreign wars and domestic unrest, and this went on for many years. In the very early months of 1642, King Louis XIII and the omnipotent actual ruler of France, Cardinal and Duke Armand de Richelieu, journeyed south to inspire the French armies to fight the Spanish for the province of Roussillon.

The Royal Upholsterers (there were several of them) served the King in turn. Poquelin the elder's period of service was during the spring months of April, May, and June. Since he was detained in Paris in 1642 by his commercial affairs, he decided to send his elder son to substitute for him in the Royal apartments. Unquestionably, he also hoped that this would acquaint Jean-Baptiste with Court life.

The son, obedient to his father's command, set out south in the early spring. At this point our hero's life is swallowed by mysterious darkness, and no one knows what precisely transpired in the south. It was rumored, however, that Jean-Baptiste took part in certain extraordinary adventures.

Cardinal Richelieu, who had the weak-willed and untalented King Louis XIII entirely in the palm of his hand, was hated by many members of the French aristocracy. In 1642 a plot was organized against the Cardinal, and the leading spirit of this plot was the young Marquis Cinq-Mars. Richelieu, a most expert politician, learned of the plot, and, although Cinq-Mars was a protégé of the King, it was decided to seize him and charge him with state treason and contacts with Spain.

On the night of June 12–13, as the rumor goes, Cinq-Mars was approached in a southern city by an unknown young man who slipped him a note. Separating himself from the other courtiers, he read the brief note in the quivering light of a torch, and hurried off in an attempt to save himself. The note read: "Your life is in danger." There was no signature.

It was said that the note had been written and delivered by the young Court Valet Poquelin, who generously sought to save Cinq-Mars from certain death. But the note merely delayed Cinq-Mars's end. He sought refuge in vain. In vain he hid in the bed of his mistress, Madame de Sioussac. He was seized on the following day, and soon executed. One hundred and eighty-four years later his memory was immortalized in a novel by Alfred de Vigny, and fifty years after de Vigny, in an opera by the famous composer of *Faust,* Charles Gounod.

Others insist, however, that there was no note, and that Jean-Baptiste had no connection whatever with the Cinq-Mars affair, but, without interfering in affairs that were none of his concern, had quietly and efficiently confined himself to the duties of Royal Valet. But then it may be asked who had invented the story of the note, and for what reason?

At the end of June the King was in Montfrin, several *lieues* away from Nîmes, and here another adventure occurred, which, as the reader shall see, will play a far more important role in our hero's life than the affair of the luckless Cinq-Mars. It was in Montfrin, at the mineral springs, that the Royal Valet, who was just completing or had just completed his term of service for that year, met once again his old friend Madeleine Béjart. The actress was touring the country with an itinerant troupe. It is not known precisely when the Royal Valet had parted ways with the King's suite. But it can be said that he did not return to Paris immediately after completing his service, that is, in July of 1642, but traveled for a time in the south—according to interested persons, in suspicious proximity to Mademoiselle Béjart. Be that as it may, in the fall of 1642 Poquelin returned to the capital and reported to his father that he had carried out his assignment.

The father inquired as to his heir's further plans. Jean-Baptiste replied that he intended to perfect himself in the knowledge of jurisprudence. At this time, as far as I know, Jean-Baptiste took up residence away from his father's house, and it was rumored in town that Poquelin's eldest son had either become a lawyer or was preparing to become one.

Anyone who took it into his head to observe how the young Poquelin was preparing for legal activities would have been greatly astonished indeed. Who had ever heard of lawyers being trained by the quacks on Pont-Neuf! Leaving the books of law at home, Jean-Baptiste had applied, in secret from his father, to one of the charlatan troupes, begging to be employed in any capacity—even that of a barker calling the public into the showbooth. Such were his studies in jurisprudence!

In later years, Jean-Baptiste's enemies—and he had a great many of them—would laugh maliciously, saying that my hero had once clowned as a dirty street farceur and swallowed snakes for the amusement of the mob. I do not know whether he swallowed snakes, but I do know that he had plunged at this time into the avid study of tragedy, and gradually began to play in amateur performances.

The reading of Corneille, which inflamed my hero's brain all through the night, the unforgettable experiences during the street performances, the odor of the stifling mask which he who had once donned it would never remove again, had finally poisoned the hapless jurist altogether, and one morning, when he snuffed out the candles over *The Cid,* he decided that the time had come for him to astonish the world.

And, indeed, he astonished the world, and the first victim of this astonishment was the long-suffering Poquelin the elder.

Chapter 7

A Brilliant Band

In the early days of January of 1643, a year rich in events, Jean-Baptiste came to his father and declared that all the plans to enter him into the Jurists' Corporation were idle dreams. He would not turn himself into a notary, he had no intention to become a scholar, and least of all did he wish to have anything to do with the upholstery shop. He would follow the calling he had been drawn to since childhood: he would become an actor.

My pen refuses to record what followed this declaration. When the father had recovered a little, he still tried to dissuade his son with every argument dictated by paternal duty. He said that the actor's profession was despised by everyone. That the Holy Church expelled actors from its bosom. That only a pauper or a tramp could lend himself to such disgrace.

The father threatened and pleaded.

"Go and think it over, I beg you, then come back and talk to me."

But the son flatly refused to reconsider anything.

Then the father rushed off to the priest and begged him with tears in his eyes to dissuade Jean-Baptiste.

The servant of God yielded to the pleas of his esteemed parishioner and attempted to bring the young man to reason. The results of his attempts were so surprising that it is even strange to record them. It was said in Paris that, after two hours of argument with the infatuated Jean-Baptiste, the servant of the Church himself discarded his black soutane and joined the same actors' company as Jean-Baptiste.

I must say that all this seems highly improbable. As far as I can remember, no priest had entered the theater, although a certain Georges Pinel had indeed pulled an odd trick with Poquelin the elder. This Georges Pinel had once, at the father's invitation, given Jean-Baptiste lessons in commercial accounting. Besides, he was connected with Poquelin through certain monetary transactions, which expressed themselves in occasional loans from the Court Upholsterer.

In despair, and not knowing where to turn, the elder Poquelin begged Pinel to speak to his former pupil. The compliant Pinel had a talk with Jean-Baptiste, after which he reported the results to the father. It turned out, in Pinel's words, that Jean-Baptiste had thoroughly convinced him, and that he, Pinel, was abandoning forever his occupation as accountant in order to become an actor along with Jean-Baptiste.

"May he be thrice cursed, this good-for-nothing Pinel! And I had lent him a hundred and fifty livres, too!" cried the unfortunate father after Pinel's departure. Then he summoned his son again.

[43]

It was the sixth day of January, a memorable day in the father's life.

"Well, do you still insist on your own way?" asked Poquelin.

"Yes, my decision is final," answered the son, in whose veins there evidently flowed the blood of the Cressés rather than the Poquelins.

"Remember," said the father, "that I shall withdraw from you the title of Royal Valet. You must return the title to me. I regret that I listened to your mad grandfather and gave you an education."

The mad and unrepentant Jean-Baptiste replied that he would willingly give up the title and had nothing against its being turned over to any of the sons his father chose.

The father demanded a written renunciation, and Jean-Baptiste signed it without a moment's thought, although, as it later transpired, it had no validity and no effect.

After that they began to divide their money. Jean-Baptiste should have received some five thousand livres inherited from his mother. His father bargained like a market woman. He could not bear to see the gold pour through the torn purses of itinerant comedians. And he was thrice right. In short, he gave his son six hundred and thirty livres, and with this sum the son walked out of his father's home.

He went directly to the Place Royale, to a certain family that was infinitely dear to his heart—the Béjarts.

Joseph Béjart, otherwise Sieur de Belleville, a petty official in the Chief Bureau of Forests and Waterways, lived in Paris with his wife, née Marie Hervé, and their four children. The entire family, from Sieur de Belleville down, was passionately devoted to the theater. The daughter Madeleine, whom we already know, was a professional actress, and an excellent one. The older son, Joseph, and the second daughter, the nineteen-year-old Geneviève, not only played in amateur theatricals, but dreamed of organizing a theater. The youngest, Louis, naturally had his heart set on following the others into the theater, and was not actively engaged in it only because of his youth—he was only thirteen. Béjart-Belleville entirely approved of his children's pursuits, and even tried to do some acting himself. Nor did the loving mother have anything against her children's passionate involvement with the theater.

It would have been difficult, indeed, to find more suitable company for Jean-Baptiste. But it was not love of the theater alone that bound Poquelin with the Béjarts. There is no question that Madeleine and Poquelin were in love and intimate with each other.

It must be noted here that the Béjart family had been journeying outside Paris from the latter part of 1641, and had returned to Paris at about the same time as our hero, by the beginning of 1643.

And so, in January of 1643, Poquelin came to the Béjarts with his legacy, and an extraordinary burst of activity ensued in the house on the Place Royale. A number of dubious young men (dubious theatrically speaking) began to frequent the Béjart home; these were followed by somewhat shopworn but experienced professional actors.

Pinel felt like a fish in water in this Bohemian company, and shone in his full glory. I would wager that no one in the world would have succeeded in the feat accomplished by Pinel. He paid a visit to Poquelin the elder and managed to wrest from him another two hundred livres for his son, about whom he told the Royal Upholsterer fantastic stories. It is said that he had behaved pretty much as Scapin had with Géronte in Molière's comedy. Everything is possible!

The preparations were completed in the summer of 1643. On June 30 a solemn agreement was drawn up at the home of the widow Marie Hervé (Sieur de Belleville had died in March of the same year). It was signed in the presence of Monsieur Marechal, attorney of the Paris Parliament. The document announced the formation of a new theater by a company of ten.

This was where the six hundred and thirty, as well as the subsequent two hundred livres had gone! Additional money for the founding of the theater was contributed by Madeleine, who was extremely thrifty and had already managed to accumulate a substantial sum during the earlier period of her stage activity. A doting mother, Marie Hervé had also scraped together her last reserves and invested her capital in the enterprise. The others, as far as can be judged, were poor as church mice, and could contribute little more than their energies and talents; as for Pinel, he brought with him his practical experience.

Without undue modesty, the company adopted the name of l'Illustre Théâtre, or the Illustrious Theater, and all its members called themselves "Children of the Family," from which we may conclude that the new servants of the muses lived in that state of harmony on which, according to Aristotle, the entire universe rests. The Children of the Family included three Béjarts, Joseph, Madeleine, and Geneviève; two young women, Malingre and des Urlis; a certain Germain Clérin; a young clerk, Bonenfant; the experienced professional actor Denys Bey; Georges Pinel; and finally, the fiery leader of the entire troupe—our Jean-Baptiste Poquelin.

Incidentally, Jean-Baptiste Poquelin ceased to exist from the moment the Illustrious Theater was formed, giving way to Jean-Baptiste Molière. Whence this new name? No one knows. Some people say that Poquelin took a stage name current among itinerant theatrical and musical circles. Others, that Jean-Baptiste called himself Molière after a certain place name. Still others, that he borrowed it from a writer who had died in 1623. But whatever the case may be, he became Molière. When his father heard about it, he threw up his hands. And Georges Pinel, in order to keep pace with his friend, assumed the name of Georges Couture.

The founding of the new company produced quite a stir in Paris, and the actors of the Hôtel de Bourgogne immediately dubbed the Children of the Family a band of ragamuffins.

The band ignored this vexation and energetically devoted itself to its business under the leadership of Molière and Bey, while Madeleine took care of the finances. To begin with, they proceeded to call on a certain Monsieur Gallois des Métayers, who leased to the band an extremely dilapidated building, formerly used for tennis games, near the Nesle Tower. Under the agreement signed with Monsieur Gallois, he undertook to renovate the hall with the aid of members of the carpenters' guild and to build a stage.

Four musicians were found and hired at twenty sol a day, and the troupe began to rehearse. When it had several plays ready, the Children of the Family piled into carts and, to lose no time while their theater was being refurbished, journeyed to the fair in Rouen to present their tragedies.

From Rouen they wrote letters to Gallois, urging him to hasten the work. After playing for a time with middling success for the undemanding audience at the Rouen fair, they returned to Paris and entered into agreement with a man of great charm, Léonard Aubry, a master of the paving trade, who undertook to lay a most magnificent pavement before the theater.

"You understand yourself, Monsieur Aubry, carriages will be driving up to the theater," Monsieur Molière said to him, rubbing his hands nervously.

He infected Monsieur Aubry with his concern, and the latter did not disappoint him: the pavement turned out to be excellent.

And, at last, on the eve of the year 1644, the theater opened with the presentation of a tragedy.

It is simply dreadful to relate what followed. I don't recall such a total failure in any other theater in the world! After the first performances, the actors of the other theaters delighted in telling everyone that not a living soul appeared in the Illustrious Theater by the moat near the Nesle Tower except the actors' parents with free passes! And alas, this is not far from the truth. All of Monsieur Aubry's efforts had been wasted: literally, not a single carriage drove up his pavement.

It began with the appearance in the neighboring Saint Sulpice parish of a certain preacher who delivered fiery sermons in competition with the performances, threatening that the devil would get into his claws not only the accursed players, but also everyone who came to see their plays.

During sleepless nights the wild thought would often visit Jean-Baptiste Molière that the best solution might be simply to cut the preacher's throat. But here I must say in defense of the preacher that he may have had nothing to do with the misfortune at all. Was it the preacher's fault that the doctor had not succeeded in curing Joseph Béjart of stuttering, and Joseph played the lovers? Was it the preacher's fault that Molière himself, who played tragic roles, also stuttered?

In the damp and gloomy hall, tallow candles burned, dripping, in cheap tin sconces. The squealing of four fiddles in no way resembled the thunder of a large orchestra. Truly brilliant dramatists stayed away from the Nesle moat, and even had they dropped in, how could the former clerk Bonenfant convey the glory of their resounding monologues?

And it went from bad to worse. What public there was behaved outrageously and permitted itself all sorts of violent outbursts, such as shouting abuse during the performance . . .

There was, of course, Madeleine, a remarkable actress, but she could not play the entire tragedy by herself! O, delightful lover of Jean-Baptiste Molière! She made every effort to save the Illustrious Theater. When her old lover, Comte de Modène, returned to Paris after a period of exile and most interesting adventures, Madeleine turned to him, and he secured for the luckless Nesle fraternity the right to call itself the Company of His Royal Highness, Gaston, Duc d'Orléans.

The cunning Jean-Baptiste Molière immediately discovered within himself the makings of a true theatrical director

[49]

and immediately engaged dancers and presented a series of ballets for the Prince's chevaliers. The chevaliers, however, remained quite indifferent toward these ballets.

Then one evening the stubborn Jean-Baptiste declared to Madeleine that the whole crux of the matter lay in the repertory, and invited Nicolas Desfontaines, actor and playwright, to join the troupe.

"What we need is a brilliant repertory," Molière said to him.

Desfontaines said that he understood Molière, and with enviable speed presented his plays to the theater. One of them was called *Perside, or the Suite of the Illustrious Basset,* another, *Saint Alexis, or the Dazzling Olympia,* a third, *The Brilliant Comedian, or the Martyrdom of Saint Genet.* But the Paris public, evidently bewitched by the preacher, showed no desire to see either the *Dazzling Olympia,* or the *Illustrious Basset.*

A slight relief was provided by the tragedy *The Family Misfortunes of Constantine the Great,* by Tristan l'Hermite, in which Madeleine played the leading role with great brilliance. But this, too, had a brief run.

When Madeleine's savings were gone, the Children of the Family went to Marie Hervé, who gave them the last of her money, crying before them for the first time.

Then they proceeded to the market, to Jean-Baptiste Poquelin the elder. A most dismal scene took place at the shop. In reply to the request for money, Poquelin at first stood speechless. And then . . . imagine, he gave it! I am certain that they must have delegated Pinel to see him.

Then Gallois put in an appearance, demanding to know

whether or not the comedians intended to pay their rent, and insisting on an unequivocal answer.

He did not receive any unequivocal answer. He received a vague reply, full of assurances and promises.

"In that case," cried Gallois, "get out! Together with your fiddles and your redhead actresses!"

The last was, of course, an overstatement, since Madeleine was the only redhead in the troupe.

"I was planning myself to get out of this wretched ditch!" shouted Molière, and the fraternity, which had never noticed how that dreadful year flew by, rushed after its commander to the Saint Paul Gates, to a hall quite similar to that of Monsieur Gallois. This hall was called the Croix-Noire, or Black Cross. The name soon justified itself.

After the illustrious company presented *Artaxerce* by the writer Jean Magnon, Monsieur de Molière, who was rightly regarded in Paris as the head of the theater, was led off to prison. He was followed by a money lender, linen merchant, and chandler called Antoine Fausset. It was he who had supplied the candles which had dripped in the sconces in Monsieur de Molière's Illustre Théâtre.

Pinel ran to Poquelin the elder.

"What? You? . . ." Jean-Baptiste Poquelin stammered, choking. "You . . . You've come again? Again to me? . . . What do you think this is?"

"He is in prison," said Pinel. "I shall not say another word, Monsieur Poquelin. He is in prison!"

The father gave him the needed money.

But at this point creditors rushed in from all sides, and Jean-Baptiste Molière would have spent the rest of his life in debtors' prison if the same Léonard Aubry who had laid the excellent and useless pavement in front of Molière's first theater had not pledged security for the debts of the Illustrious Theater.

I do not know what potions Georges Pinel fed Léonard Aubry, but may the name of Léonard Aubry go down into posterity!

After the leader of the Illustrious Theater had left prison, the entire troupe solemnly promised Monsieur Aubry to pay off the debts he had vouched for.

With Molière's return, the performances were resumed. Molière managed to win the patronage of Henri de Lorraine, Duc de Guise, and the company received a most generous gift from the Duke—his large and elegant wardrobe. The fraternity donned the luxurious suits, and pawned the gold-embroidered ribbons. But even the ribbons were of small avail. The brotherhood was shaken. The first symptoms of panic began to appear. It became necessary to abandon the Saint Paul Gates and the sepulchral Black Cross, and to move to a new hall. This hall had a more cheerful name— White Cross.

Alas! It turned out to be no better than the Black Cross.

The first to escape, unable to face any more privations, were Pinel, Bonenfant, and later Bey. The painful agony of the Illustre Théâtre went on for some time longer, but by the beginning of 1645 everything was clear. All that could have been sold was sold: costumes, sets . . .

In the fall of 1645, the theater ceased its existence forever.

That was in the fall. One evening a woman sat in the tiny, crowded apartment on rue des Jardin Saint Paul, lit by a single candle. A man stood before her. Three difficult years, debts, usurers, prison, and humiliation had wrought sharp changes in him. Hard experience had traced bitter lines at the corners of his lips, but a close look at his face was sufficient to make it clear that no misfortunes could stop this man. He could never become a lawyer, a notary, or a furniture merchant. Before the red-haired Madeleine stood a hardened professional actor of twenty-four, who had gone through fire and water. The remnants of Guise's caftan hung from his shoulders, and, as he paced the room, his last few sous clinked in his pockets.

The head of the Illustrious Theater, flat broke, went over to the window and heaped curses of consummate eloquence on Paris, all its suburbs, its Black and its White Crosses, and its ditch by the Nesle Tower. Then he proceeded to pile abuse upon the Paris public, which had no inkling of what art was, and added that there was only one decent man in Paris, and that was the Royal paver, Léonard Aubry.

He babbled on for a long time, receiving no answer, and finally asked in despair:

"And now, of course, you too will abandon me? Well, you can go and try to join the Hôtel de Bourgogne."

And he added that all the members of the Bourgogne company were scoundrels.

The red-haired Madeleine heard out all this nonsense, was silent for a while, and then the lovers began to whisper with one another. Their whispered conversation went on till morning, but what they finally agreed on no one knows.

Chapter 8

The Itinerant Player

Unfortunately, it is totally unknown where my hero went at this point. He disappeared from Paris and seemed to have vanished from the earth. For a year not a word was to be heard of him, but later rather dubious witnesses began to say that in the summer of 1647 a man bearing a remarkable resemblance to the bankrupt theater director Molière had been seen in the street in Rome. He was standing, they said, under the scorching sun, conversing respectfully with the French Ambassador, Monsieur de Fontenay-Mareuil.

In the autumn of the same year important events took place in Naples. A brave fisherman, Tommasso Anniello, led a popular uprising against the Duc d'Arcos, the Spanish Vice-Regent who ruled Naples at the time. Pistol shots were heard in the streets, and the pavements were reddened with blood. Tommasso was captured and executed, and his head was raised on a lance, but the Neapolitan people buried him in solemn ceremony, placing a sword and a marshal's baton in his coffin.

After this the French intervened in the Neapolitan conflict, and Henri II de Lorraine, Duc de Guise, appeared with troops in Naples.

And it was said that the former director of the luckless l'Illustre Théâtre, Monsieur de Molière, was a member of Guise's suite. Why he was there or what he did in Naples was not explained by anyone.

Others, however, insisted that Jean-Baptiste had never been either in Rome or in Naples, and that he had simply been confused with another young man of adventurous bent.

In fact, there were witnesses who testified to something entirely different. Namely, that in the summer of 1646 a shabby caravan had left Paris and, crossing the suburb of Saint-Germain, proceeded to the south of France. Carts loaded with dilapidated belongings were drawn by scrawny oxen. In the first cart sat a redheaded woman, wrapped in a cloak against the dust. This woman, it was said, was none other than Madeleine Béjart. If this is so, we must remember and honor her name. The bewitching actress had not abandoned her lover in a difficult moment, when he had lost his first battle in Paris. She had made no attempt to join either the Theater on the Swamp or the Bourgogne theater. She no longer made any cunning plans to catch her first lover, Comte de Modène, in her net and get him to marry her. She was a strong and loyal woman, and everyone should know it!

Next to the cart limped a boy of about sixteen, and street urchins in the villages they passed through whistled and taunted him:

"Lame devil!"

And after a closer look they added:

"Cross-eyed too! Cross-eyed too!"

And, indeed, Louis Béjart was lame and cross-eyed.

When the clouds of dust subsided a little, other people could be recognized in the carts. Their faces were familiar: the tragic lover and stutterer Joseph Béjart, his quarrelsome sister Geneviève . . .

The caravan was led, as may easily be guessed, by Jean-Baptiste Molière.

In short, when the Illustrious Theater perished, Molière brought out from under the ruins the remnants of the loyal fraternal company and put them on wheels.

This man could not exist a single moment outside the theater, and he had enough spiritual strength to take to the road as an itinerant comedian after three years of work in Paris. But that was not all. As you see, his fiery speeches convinced the entire Béjart family to follow him. And, thanks to him, all the Béjarts now found themselves enveloped in the dust of the French roads. Together with the Béjarts, some new faces were to be seen in the company, including the professional tragedian Charles Dufresne, who was also a scene painter and director and had at one time headed his own company. There was also the professional comic actor René Berthelot, or du Parc, who was soon dubbed Gros-René, a nickname he retained for the rest of his life, because he played the roles of funny fat servants.

In his own cart, the leader of the caravan had plays by l'Hermite, Magnon, and Corneille.

At first, the wanderers had a difficult time. They often had to sleep in haylofts and play in villages in wooden barns, putting up dirty rags in place of curtains. Sometimes, however, they found themselves in wealthy castles, and, if the titled owner was bored enough to express a wish to see the comedians, Molière's actors, grimy and sweaty from the road, played in the reception chambers.

Arriving at a new place, the actors began by respectfully removing their shabby hats and visiting the local authorities for permission to play before the people. The local authorities, as was to be expected, treated the comedians with hostility and contempt and raised numberless difficulties in their way.

The actors would say that they wished to present a tragedy in verse by the most esteemed Monsieur Corneille. I doubt that the local authorities had any notion of Corneille's verse. Nevertheless, they demanded to see the script and, having seen it, often forbade its performance, giving a variety of reasons. The most frequent of these reasons was:

"Our people are poor, and there is no need for them to waste money on your shows."

There were also enigmatic answers, such as "We are afraid that your shows may lead to trouble. . . ."

But there were encouraging answers too; one never knew what to expect in that gypsy existence.

The clergy responded to the players with uniform disapproval, and the company often had to resort to wiles such as offering to contribute the receipts of the first performance to the local monastery or for philanthropic needs. This often saved the show.

On arriving in a town, the company first looked for a gambling house or a barn for ball games, of which the Frenchmen were fond. After coming to an agreement with the owner, they would contrive a makeshift stage, don their shabby costumes, and play.

They slept at inns, at times two or three in a bed.

And so they made their way through France, looping back and forth. There was a rumor that Molière's comedians had been seen in Le Mans early in their wanderings.

In 1647 the company came to the city of Bordeaux, in the province of Guienne, the home of the excellent Bordeaux wines. Here the sun smiled on the comedians, who had grown lean in their journeyings. Officially, Guienne was governed by Bernard de Nogaret, Duc d'Épernon. However, everybody knew that the real governor of the province was a certain Ninon de Lartiges, and Guienne suffered a great deal at the hands of this lady.

But it so happened that, wearied by the labors of governing, Madame de Lartiges fell into a melancholy, and the Duc d'Épernon decided to arrange a series of entertainments and diversions for her on the Garonne River. Molière's arrival in Guienne was most opportune! The Duke received the players with open arms, and the pleasant clink of gold was heard for the first time in their pockets.

Molière and his troupe played for the Duke and his mistress Magnon's tragedy *Jehosophat* and other plays. It is rumored that, besides these, they performed yet another work of art which demands mention. This was a tragedy, *The Thebans,* said to have been composed by Molière himself during his wanderings, and also said to have been an extremely inept work.

In the spring of 1648 our comedians were already elsewhere, namely, in the city of Nantes, where they left a trace in the official records, from which it may be seen that a certain "Morlièrre" had requested permission to present theatrical performances, which permission was granted. It is also known that in Nantes Molière encountered a rival company, the marionettes of the Venetian Segale, and that Molière's troupe emerged victorious over the marionettes. Segale was obliged to cede the city to Molière.

The summer and winter of 1648 were spent by the company in towns and villages in the vicinity of Nantes, and in the spring of 1649 it moved to Limoges, where it was given a most vexing reception: Monsieur de Molière, performing in one of his tragic roles, was cruelly hooted down by the local audience, which also pelted him with baked apples to express its disapproval of his acting.

Cursing Limoges, Monsieur de Molière led his wandering fraternity elsewhere. The troupe visited Angoulême, Agen, and Toulouse. And in January of 1650 they came to Narbonne. In the spring of that year, Monsieur de Molière temporarily left the company for a secret visit to Paris.

It is known that in the winter of 1650 Molière and his troupe came to Pézenas, where he left a trace of his visit in the form of a receipt for four thousand livres he had been issued for his company at the order of the members of the Estates, who had assembled in Pézenas to discuss important questions of taxation. The receipt is unquestionable evidence that Molière had given performances for the members of the Estates.

In the spring of 1651 Molière visited Paris again, where he borrowed from his father one thousand nine hundred and seventy-five livres, after proving to him that without this money he was a finished man, for he still had to pay some of the debts of the Illustrious Theater. Having paid his creditors in Paris, he rejoined his troupe for further wandering.

At this time a rather important fact came to light: Monsieur de Molière discovered that he was drawn not only to performing in plays, but also to composing them himself. Despite his superhuman work during the day, Molière began to sit up nights writing plays. And it is somewhat strange that this man, who had devoted himself to the study of tragedies and was considered a tragic actor, did not return to tragedy after the unfortunate *Thebans,* but began instead to turn out gay, rollicking one-act farces in imitation of the Italians, who were great masters of this genre. The farces were enthusiastically received by Molière's companions, and became a part of the repertory. And the greatest success in the performance of these farces fell to the lot of Molière himself, who played comic roles—chiefly those of Sganarelle.

One might well ask where Molière had learned this art of being funny on the stage. At the time when the ill-fated l'Illustre Théâtre was being formed, or perhaps a little earlier, there appeared in Paris, among other Italian actors, the most famous and talented performer of the Italian masked character Scaramuccio, or Scaramouche—Tiberio Fiorillo. Dressed in black from head to foot, with only a white pleated collar, Scaramouche astonished all Paris with his virtuoso antics and brilliant performance in the frothy, comic Italian farces.

The beginning actor Jean-Baptiste Poquelin came to Scaramouche and asked to be given lessons in the art of acting. Scaramouche agreed. It was unquestionably from him that Molière had learned his knack for comic roles and a taste for farces.

And so, the leader of the itinerant troupe played tragic roles in tragedies by other authors, and comic roles in his own farces. And here another circumstance became apparent, to the endless astonishment of our hero. In tragic roles he had at best a fair to middling success, and at worst a total fiasco. And it must regretfully be admitted that the latter happened quite often. Alas, it was not only in Limoges that the poor tragedian was pelted with apples as he paraded on the stage in the coronet of some noble hero!

But as soon as farce followed tragedy, and Molière transformed himself from Caesar into Sganarelle, there was an immediate change: the audience roared with laughter, applauded, and gave him ovations, and the townsmen came in droves to the succeeding performances.

Removing his makeup after the show, or taking off his mask, Molière would stutter in his dressing room:

"Idiots, may they be thrice damned! I can't understand it. . . . What is wrong with Corneille's plays?"

"No, no," his colleagues would say to the puzzled director, "Corneille's plays are excellent, but . . ."

"If it were only the rabble, I could understand it. . . . The rabble needs farces. But the gentry! After all, there are educated people among them! I don't see how anyone could laugh at this folderol! I wouldn't even smile at it!"

"Ah, Monsieur de Molière!" his colleagues would reply. "People long for laughter, and it is just as easy to amuse a courtier as a common man!"

"So, they want farces?" cried the former Poquelin. "Very well! We shall give them farces!"

Then followed the usual story: fiasco in tragedy, and success in farce.

But how is this to be explained? Why did the tragedian fail where the comedian succeeded? There can be only one answer to this, and a very simple one. It was not the world that was blind, as Molière, who considered himself clear-sighted, concluded, but quite the opposite: the world had perfect eyesight, and only Monsieur de Molière was blind. And strangely enough, for a very long time. He alone among all around him failed to understand that he had been extraordinarily fortunate to be trained by Scaramouche, because he had an inborn genius for comedy, and no talent whatsoever for tragedy. And neither the gentle hints of Madeleine nor the roundabout suggestions of his colleagues were of any avail: the commander of the troupe stubbornly persisted in playing roles for which he was entirely unfit.

This was one of the reasons for the fiasco of the Illustrious Theater! It was clearly Molière's fault, and not the fault of the preacher at Saint Sulpice. And it was not his stuttering alone, although everyone remarked on it, for the dedicated actor succeeded, by dint of persistent exercises, in almost eliminating this speech defect, as well as his incorrect breathing. The trouble was in his total lack of talent for tragedy.

But let us follow Molière's caravan further. A rumor spread from village to village, from town to town in southern France, that a young fellow, a certain Molière, had appeared in the region with his company of players, and that they performed brilliantly in comic plays. The only incorrect part of this rumor was that Molière was a young fellow. When people began to talk about him, he was thirty years old. And this thirty-year-old actor and playwright, tempered by bitter experience and increasingly admired and trusted by his company, was at the end of 1652 approaching Lyons, bringing with him, in addition to several farces, a full-length comedy called *The Bungler*.

The caravan approached Lyons with confidence. The actors were sufficiently seasoned. They now wore fine caftans, their carriages bulged with theatrical properties and personal belongings. The actors no longer trembled to think of what might await them in Lyons. The power of Molière's farces was well known to them, and they liked *The Bungler* very well indeed. They were not intimidated at the sight of the enormous city that emerged before them out of the winter fog.

In one of the carts, under the tireless care of Madeleine, there was a new individual, who had joined the caravan in the vicinity of Nîmes. This person, only ten years old, was a homely, but vivacious, clever, and coquettish little girl.

Madeleine explained the sudden appearance of this girl by telling the actors that she was her sister, who had been cared for by a lady of her acquaintance who lived near Nîmes, and had now come to live with Madeleine. Monsieur de Molière, she said, was also very fond of her and intended to teach her. The girl would become an actress, playing under the name of Menou.

A little surprised by the sudden appearance of this young sister of their colleague, the enchanting Madeleine, the company gossiped a while, wondering why she had been brought up in the provinces rather than Paris. But before long the actors became accustomed to the girl, and Menou became a member of the family of wandering players.

The actors had not been mistaken about *The Bungler*. The play was performed in January of 1653, and met with extraordinary success. It was the Lyons indoor ball court that would have benefited from a new pavement by the trusting Léonard Aubry! Monsieur de Molière had been too hasty, in his youthful enthusiasm, with paving the street by the Nesle ditch.

After the premiere the public rushed to the box office in droves. On one occasion two gentlemen quarreled bitterly amid the crush, and later fought a duel. In short, the public besieged Molière's theater, and a rival troupe led by a certain Mitalla was practically wiped out of existence.

Madly cursing that upstart Molière, Mitalla dissolved his company, and his best players came to offer their services to Molière.

The most valuable gift Molière received from Monsieur Mitalla, whom he had ruined with his *The Bungler,* was Catherine Leclerc du Rozet, known by her married name of de Brie. When she came to Molière, he engaged her immediately to play female leads, since she was known as an excellent actress. Madame de Brie recommended her husband, Monsieur de Brie, who played bullies, and he was accepted into the troupe despite his being a second-rate actor. It was a small price to pay for Catherine de Brie.

She was followed by the very young, but already famous, Mademoiselle de Gorla, who created a sensation wherever she performed. Marquise-Thérèse de Gorla, daughter of a showbooth comedian, had herself appeared in showbooth performances from her earliest childhood and very early became a first-rate tragedienne and an inimitable dancer.

The members of Molière's company were tremendously impressed with Marquise-Thérèse: all the actors were captivated by her beauty and her dancing. She turned the head of every man who saw her.

The appearance of de Brie and de Gorla was a heavy blow to Madeleine. Until then she had had no rivals in the troupe.

In Lyons two appeared at once, and both extremely strong. Madeleine realized that she would have to surrender the leads to them. And, indeed, this was so. With the coming of the Lyons stars, Madeleine was relegated to the playing of soubrettes. The female romantic leads went to de Brie, and the tragic leads were assigned to Marquise-Thérèse.

Another wound sustained by Madeleine was equally deep. Jean-Baptiste was the first to be smitten by the beauty of Marquise-Thérèse. He became violently infatuated and began to seek a return of affection. And Madeleine, who had endured all the hardships of their nomadic existence, was now compelled to witness Molière's romance. It proved unsuccessful. The great actress and dancer rejected Molière and, surprising everyone with her choice, married the fat du Parc. Nevertheless, Molière never returned to Madeleine. The romance with Thérèse was immediately followed by another, with Madame de Brie, and this time it was successful. The gentle and sweet de Brie, the very opposite of the haughty and cruel Marquise-Thérèse, was for many years Molière's secret mistress.

When the first passions died down, when all the relationships were reshuffled, and when the bitterness of the first nocturnal scenes between the offended Madeleine and Molière had abated to some extent, the enlarged company became widely active in Lyons and its environs. *The Bungler* was always a triumph. Among the other plays, we may mention Corneille's *Andromède,* in which the girl Menou made her first appearance in the tiny role of Éphyre and handled her role, with several lines of text, very well indeed.

Chapter 9

Prince de Conti Makes His Entry Upon the Stage

While our wandering troupe was peacefully traveling from town to town, many events took place in France. Neither the all-powerful Cardinal Richelieu, nor King Louis XIII, who had been his obedient puppet, were any longer among the living. Richelieu died late in 1642, soon after the chevalier Cinq-Mars was put to death, and King Louis XIII departed this earth in May, 1643, after uttering his final words, "My spirit is bowed with the weight of my life."

A new King ruled France, but this King was only several years old.

Louis XIV was born in October of 1638. Cannon shots and the light of smoking lampions announced to the world the arrival of a new Louis. When his father, Louis XIII, died, the young King's mother, Queen Anne of Austria, assumed the reins. But she was a regent on paper only, while the actual power was in the hands of another Cardinal and Prime Minister of France, the Sicilian Julio Mazarini, or Jules Mazarin.

History seemed to repeat itself. The highest French aristocracy, whose representatives had formerly opposed Richelieu, now declared itself against the new Minister. The opposition became known as the Fronde. The anti-government outbreaks lasted some five years.

Prince Condé the Great, an exceptionally talented general who had by then won many laurels and who played a leading role in the Fronde, had on a number of occasions switched to the government's side in pursuit of his personal interests. After a five-year struggle, Mazarin emerged victorious. Condé had lost. He left France and went over to the Spaniards, and the Cardinal made a triumphal entry into Paris.

Young as he was, Louis understood very well the significance of events during the existence of the Fronde, and he retained throughout his life a clear memory of how the French aristocracy had almost robbed him of the throne.

As regards Condé's subsequent history, it must be added that he made peace with Mazarin several years later, and was pardoned.

Prince de Conti, brother of Condé, whom we knew as a boy when he was a student at the Collège de Clermont, had by the time of the Fronde grown into a young man preparing for priesthood. However, instead of renouncing all mundane concerns as he was preparing for the highest of all careers, Conti, who was known for instability and impulsiveness, followed his great brother and participated in the Fronde. And not only did he take part in bloody battles, but he also sat for a time in prison.

By the end of the summer of 1653, Conti had quietly retired to his château at La Grange, near Pézenas, in blessed Languedoc, and was even entrusted temporarily with the duties of governor of Languedoc.

While the Prince was resting at his château, our players, unaffected by the storm of the Fronde which had swept across the country, were traveling in Languedoc, and fate chose to bring the two Clermont alumni together.

A certain Madame de Calvimont was visiting at the time at the Conti château. She was a captivating lady with but a single blemish, according to general opinion—her extraordinary stupidity. Strolling through the magnificent parks, barely touched by the yellow of August, Madame de Calvimont complained to the Prince about the absence of any entertainments in the château. In reply, the Prince said everything that is commonly said on such occasions, namely that to him the lady's wishes were law. And he immediately summoned his closest attendant, Monsieur de Cosnac, a most charming and cultivated man.

Daniel de Cosnac knew of Molière's presence in Languedoc and of the great success he was enjoying. He sent a messenger at once with orders to seek out the director of the troupe and convey to him an invitation from His Highness to come with the entire company to La Grange.

Needless to say, the former Clermont student and present comedian did not wait to be asked twice. He instantly discontinued performances, loaded the company with all its properties and accessories into wagons, and the caravan proceeded to the Prince's château.

In the meantime, another itinerant troupe, uninvited by anyone, had approached the castle. It was led by the veteran street charlatan, tooth-puller, and actor, Monsieur Cormier, who had once plied his trades on Pont-Neuf in Paris.

When the Prince was informed of the arrival of a troupe of actors, he was most pleasantly surprised at the magical speed with which he was able to meet Madame de Calvimont's wish. And, without waiting for any Molière, he bade his servants to invite the troupe into the château.

The troupe launched its activities in the château, and the experienced Cormier instantly realized that his fate at the moment depended on pleasing Madame de Calvimont. He showered her with flatteries, and even gifts.

But before Cormier had had time to expand to the full and forget for a time the privations of the road, Daniel Cosnac was informed that Molière and his caravan had arrived at his invitation. He went to report to the Prince that the director and the company His Highness had invited were at the gates, and asked for instructions.

After a moment's thought, the Prince said that Monsieur Molière could consider himself free, since his performances were no longer required.

"But, Your Highness," said Cosnac, turning pale, "I invited him . . ."

"And I, as you see," replied the Prince, "invited Cormier, and you will surely agree that it would be more appropriate for you to break your word rather than for me to break mine."

Cosnac slowly went out to make his excuses to the newly arrived Molière.

Before the entrance to the château stood a man with full lips and tired eyes. His clothes were covered with dust, and his traveling boots were literally white with it.

Beyond the gates of the château could be seen a long caravan. However, Cosnac did not look closely either at the man or at his caravan; he was afraid to lift his eyes.

"I am Molière," the man said in a slightly hoarse voice, removing his hat. "We have come at the invitation of His Highness."

Cosnac, filling his lungs with air and scarcely able to move his tongue, mumbled:

"The Prince . . . instructed me . . . to tell Monsieur Molière . . . that there has been a lamentable misunderstanding. . . . Another company is already playing in the château. . . . The Prince begs you to consider yourself . . . He asked me to tell you that you are free."

There was a silence.

The visitor stepped back without removing his eyes from Cosnac, and replaced his hat. Cosnac raised his eyes and saw him turning pale. The silence continued.

Then the visitor began, his eyes crossed to the tip of his nose:

"But I was invited . . . I . . ." He pointed at his wagons. "I canceled performances, I loaded our sets, I have women, actresses with me."

Cosnac was silent.

"I must ask," said the visitor, beginning to stutter, "that I be paid at least a thousand écu. I have suffered great losses, I broke off performances and transported people."

Cosnac wiped the sweat off his brow and humbly asked the visitor to sit down on a bench and wait while he reported his request to the Prince.

The other backed away silently, sat down on a bench, and

[70]

lowered his eyes to the ground. Cosnac went back to the Prince's apartments.

"He asks for a thousand écu, to compensate him for expenses," said Cosnac.

"What nonsense!" said the Prince. "I don't owe him anything. And I must ask you not to bring up the subject to me again, I am tired of it."

Cosnac left the Prince, went to his own room, took one thousand écu of his own money, and brought it to Molière. The latter thanked him and put the money into a leather pouch. Cosnac began to apologize: he was extremely sorry that everything had turned out so awkwardly. . . . And suddenly, on an inspiration, he suggested that Molière stop in the nearby town of Pézenas, and give his performances there. He would arrange everything, get him a hall and a permit . . .

Monsieur de Molière thought it over and agreed. And Cosnac went to Pézenas with the caravan, obtained a hall and a permit in the name of the Prince, and the company presented *The Bungler,* dazzling the local public with their art.

Rumors of the unprecedented performance immediately reached the ears of the Governor. And the Prince declared that he wished to see those excellent players in his château.

Comedians cannot afford to remember grievances, and the former Clermont student did not delay in bringing his company to the château. *The Bungler* was performed in the presence of the Prince, his suite, and Madame de Calvimont —to the despair of the unfortunate Cormier. There was no question at all of his continuing at the château. His shabbily dressed and inept comedians could not dream of competing with the du Parcs, de Bries, Madeleine, and, of course, Molière himself in the rich costumes they had acquired after the Lyons successes.

And yet, it is just possible that Molière would, after all, have had to leave, yielding the field to Cormier, for the performance delighted everyone, with the sole exception of Madame de Calvimont. Fortunately, the clever and cultivated secretary of the Prince, the poet Sarrazin, saved the day. He was so vociferously enthusiastic about the acting and costumes of the players, so persuasive in his argument that the company would be an adornment to the Prince's Court, that the capricious Prince ordered the luckless Cormier dismissed and Molière's company invited to take up permanent service with him, naturally with a regular allowance and with the right to call itself the Court Troupe of Armand de Bourbon, Prince de Conti.

It must be added that Sarrazin's praises of Molière's troupe were partly attributable to the fact that he had fallen instantly in love with Marquise-Thérèse.

The poor Cormier and his comedians went away, cursing Molière, but truly golden days followed for the latter and his company in Languedoc.

The wily stutterer seemed to have bewitched the Prince. Performances went on continuously, and all manner of benefits flowed as continuously to Molière and his players. When they had to travel in Languedoc, the Prince obligingly requisitioned horses and wagons for the transportation of the actors and the equipment, the Prince gave them money, the Prince extended them full patronage.

In November of 1653 the Prince journeyed to Paris via

Lyons to marry Mazarin's niece, Marie Anne Martinozzi. The Court company escorted the Prince to Lyons, where it remained for performances, while the Prince went on to Paris, married Martinozzi, and returned to Languedoc early in 1654.

In December of 1654 the Estates met in the town of Montpellier. The gentry and the clergy assembled, as usual, to discuss financial questions with the representatives of the central government, and to defend, as far as possible, the interests of the province. The Deputies, who received most considerable allowances during the meeting of the Estates, were very fond of this period. Generally, wherever the Estates met, life always quickened. And, of course, Molière's company appeared in Montpellier to play for the assembled gentry.

Only one member of the Prince's suite was not destined to admire either the dazzling Deputies or Monsieur de Molière's performances. This was the Prince's secretary, Monsieur de Sarrazin. He had died of hectic fever in December of 1654.

Sarrazin's death led the Prince to make a rather astonishing offer to Molière. He asked him to become his secretary in place of the late Sarrazin. Molière had a difficult time declining this flattering offer in the most tactful form: he said that he was organically incapable of serving as a secretary. Fortunately, the Prince was not offended, and the company launched its performances in Montpellier.

Well acquainted by now with the Prince's tastes, Molière collaborated with Joseph Béjart in composing the libretto of a ballet with a gay divertissement. The ballet was performed in December for the Prince and Princess, and

[73]

the greatest success in the entertainment fell to its initiator, Monsieur de Molière, whose performance in the role of a market woman selling herrings provoked thunderous peals of laughter.

And Joseph Béjart, in addition to the success he had won with his couplets, had yet another stroke of luck. The always painstaking and attentive Joseph, who had a penchant for historical research, had prepared a detailed compilation of a heraldic nature, which included a variety of genealogical data, as well as descriptions of the coats of arms and devices of the barons and prelates of the Languedoc Estates assembled in 1654.

Béjart had, naturally, dedicated the compilation to the Prince, who had obtained a respectable sum of money for it from the esteemed Deputies, accompanied, it is true, with hints that it would be preferable that Béjart composed such documents only when he had been commissioned to do so.

When the Estates had completed their assembly in Montpellier, Molière moved with his company to Lyons, where a most remarkable man made his appearance among the players. His name was Charles Coypeau d'Assouci, and he was already past fifty. D'Assouci wandered through France with his lute accompanied by two boys, with whom he sang songs and couplets of his own composition, and called himself the Emperor of Entertainers. All the money he earned was left by the itinerant poet and musician d'Assouci in gambling houses and taverns.

The summer of 1655 had been particularly unlucky for him. Some card sharps had cleaned him out to the last sou, leaving him nothing but his lute and the two boys. Being thus stranded in Lyons, d'Assouci presented himself to Molière to express his pleasure in meeting the artists and to pay them a brief visit. This visit lasted some twelve months.

What interests us most is d'Assouci's enthusiastic testimony to the improved circumstances of Molière's fraternity. During the two years of Conti's patronage, they had earned a good deal of money, the actors' shares had risen, and they had forgotten the cold nights in haylofts and the humiliating obeisances to the local authorities. Molière and his fellow actors and actresses lived in excellent quarters in Lyons, they had sufficient stocks of wine, they were very well dressed, had acquired confidence in themselves, and showed limitless good nature.

The actors liked the Emperor of Entertainers, and he went to live with them as one of the company. In return, he eulogized them in his best lines of prose and poetry.

"People say," d'Assouci would declaim on street corners, "that the best of brothers would get tired of feeding his own brother for more than a month. But these people, I assure you, are far more noble than all brothers taken together!"

And d'Assouci sang his verses, which rhymed "company" and "harmony," and which invariably mentioned that he, a pauper, sat at the fraternity's table every day, and partook of its seven- or eight-course dinners. The best time at these dinners came after the eighth course, when the irrepressible Emperor filled all the glasses with wine and began to sing, together with Molière, song after gay song, or else told comic tales. In short, those were marvelous days in Lyons!

When the players moved on to Avignon in the autumn

of 1655, d'Assouci naturally went with them. The fraternity sailed down the Rhone in barks, the stars lighted its way, and d'Assouci sat in the stern, playing his many-stringed lute till late in the night.

After a month in Avignon, the troupe was summoned by the Prince to Pézenas, to another session of the Estates.

On November 9 the Deputies witnessed an extraordinary incident. Apartments for His Highness Prince de Conti were prepared in the house of a certain Monsieur d'Alfonce. The bishops of nearby towns in full regalia and mantles, and with them the representatives of the gentry, the Barons de Villeneuve and de Lanta, in gala attire, presented themselves at the d'Alfonce house to greet His Highness.

The Prince came out to see the Deputies, but received them in the door of the vestibule, begging their indulgence and explaining that, unfortunately, he could not admit them within, since the rooms were in complete disarray—Monsieur de Molière just having presented a comedy.

It is difficult to describe the faces of the Deputies and, particularly, of the bishops. But, naturally, no one said anything to the Prince and, conveying its compliments to His Highness, the delegation departed in stony silence.

The troupe played in Pézenas for several months, and Molière received six thousand livres from the treasury of the Languedoc Estates.

Molière's stay in Pézenas was marked by several strange actions. For example, he cultivated a friendship with the best local wigmaker, Maître Gély.

Gély's establishment enjoyed great popularity in Pézenas, especially on Saturdays. The door opened and closed continually, admitting butchers, bakers, Pézenas officials, and sundry other people. While Maître Gély's assistants pulled teeth or shaved the customers, others awaited their turn, chatting and taking snuff. From time to time a young woman would come running in and declare, blushing, that she had received a letter from her sweetheart in the army. Everyone participated in this event, and the letter was read aloud for the illiterate girl, with exclamations of approval at good news, and sympathy if the news was bad. In short, Maître Gély's establishment was also a kind of club.

And so, Molière had volunteered to assist Gély on Saturdays in counting the take in the cash box. The hospitable Gély offered the director a wooden armchair by the counter, and the latter sat in it, receiving the silver coins. Maître Gély, however, would whisper in secret that the take had nothing to do with Molière's presence, that it was merely a pretext for other activities: the director of the Conti troupe always carried a supply of clean sheets of paper under the flaps of his caftan, on which he jotted down everything of interest that was said at the shop. But the reason for the director's actions was not known to Maître Gély.

Be that as it may, the wooden armchair from the barber shop subsequently found its way into a museum.

During its stay in Pézenas, the troupe occasionally visited neighboring villages, and in the spring of 1656 it proceeded to the city of Narbonne, where the gay troubadour d'Assouci finally left it. After that, the comedians went to Lyons, their permanent residence, and from there to the town of Béziers to entertain another assembly of Estates.

At Béziers Molière presented the premiere of his new play, which he called *The Amorous Quarrel*. This was a five-act play, written under the evident influence of Spanish and Italian playwrights. It was technically better than *The Bungler*, but its verse was occasionally heavy, and its finale very complicated and rather implausible. But since the weaker parts were submerged in the mass of witty and subtle scenes, the players expected a great success, and they were not mistaken.

On arriving in Béziers, the director of the theater began his run by sending free tickets to the premiere to all the Deputies of the Estates, who replied to the courtesy by a terrible affront: the miserly Deputies returned the tickets. The reason for this was clear. The Deputies knew that after a time the troupe would appeal for a financial subsidy, and they decided to prevent this from the outset. The director realized that he would probably no longer have the opportunity to sign any receipts for some thousands of livres from the treasury of the Estates. With the usual mental curses at the address of the Deputies, Molière presented the play before an ordinary audience. And the audience drowned out *The Amorous Quarrel*, in which Molière played Albert, the father, with applause.

Leaving the inhospitable Béziers, Molière made another visit to Lyons, where he performed the play with brilliant success. From there he went on to Nîmes, Orange, and Avignon.

In 1657 two meetings took place in Avignon. The director met his old friend and Clermont fellow student Chapelle. The former pupils of the philosopher Gassendi embraced tenderly. They exchanged recollections of the Epicurean and talked about his grievous end at the hands of his accursed physicians, who thought to cure every ill by bloodletting.

The second meeting played an enormous role in Molière's subsequent life. The famed painter Pierre Mignard had stopped in Avignon on his way back from Italy. When they met, Molière and Mignard immediately liked each other and quickly became friends. The brilliant portraitist painted Molière in several poses.

The summer of 1657 was unusually hot, and the troupe went north to Dijon for a time, returning to Lyons for the winter. And the two old Clermont alumni, Prince de Conti and Molière, who had not seen one another for a rather long time, once again found themselves in close proximity. The director of the troupe joyfully addressed himself to the Prince, but this time the two did not meet. The Prince not only refused to see the director and his players, but even issued orders forbidding the company the use of his name. The life of comedians does not consist of roses and laurels alone! The humiliated director waited for explanations, and they were soon forthcoming. It transpired that His Highness had undergone a complete change of heart during the two preceding years. The former Frondeur and then passionate devotee of the theater was now surrounded by clergy and immersed in the study of religious and moral problems.

One of the bishops who was particularly eloquent had turned his attention to the Prince's love of the theater and urgently suggested to him that, no matter how high a man's position in the world, his first concern should be for the salvation of his soul. And the first thing to do was to shun comedians and their performances as one would shun fire, lest the soul should later find itself in fire eternal. The bishop's words bore abundant fruit. Conti adopted the bishop's advice and declared to his attendants that from then on he would not venture even to set his eyes upon comedians.

"How inconstant are the mighty of this world," Molière said to Madeleine. "And I would give this advice to all players: if you happen to win favor, seize everything you can at once. Lose no time, strike while the iron is hot. And leave of your own choice, don't wait till you are thrown out! . . . And generally, Madeleine, we have to put our minds to more important things. I think it is time for us to leave Languedoc. We should now . . ."

And again, as once upon a time in Paris, after the collapse of the Illustrious Theater, the former lovers went into a whispered conference.

Chapter 10
Look Out, Bourgogne—
Molière Is Coming!

The winter of 1657 was generally a time of high excitement in the company. The actors were always whispering among themselves. There were constant mysterious discussions between Molière and Madeleine, the troupe's financial genius. Madeleine had many talks with various business people connected with Paris. But no one in the company knew precisely what was going on.

Early in 1658 the troupe moved to Grenoble, where it played during the carnival. Then it visited Lyons for the last time. And suddenly Molière took it, without stopping anywhere, to Rouen. His caravan passed a short distance away from Paris, but did not even turn in its direction. And it came to Rouen, where fifteen years earlier it had made an appearance with the inexperienced Children of the Family to play at the Rouen fair.

But this time the circumstances were entirely different. This time the visitor was a man of thirty-six, a most experienced actor and a first-rate comedian. And he brought with him a company of excellent players. Among the women

[81]

of the troupe there were genuine stars: Madeleine Béjart, Catherine de Brie, and Marquise-Thérèse du Parc. The once-shabby company which had with difficulty won a victory in Nantes over the Venetian's wretched marionettes now strode across France, putting every other itinerant troupe it met confidently into the shade. In the south it left in its wake the trampled Mitalla and Cormier, and in the north Molière's arrival was awaited with trepidation by the director of another troupe playing in Rouen, Philibert Gassot, Sieur du Croisy.

The rumor of Molière's approach spread through Rouen like fire. Molière entered Rouen, rented the Hall of Two Moors, and opened his performances. One of the most important events that occurred in Rouen was the meeting between Molière and the greatest French playwright, Pierre Corneille, whose plays had long been a part of Molière's repertory. And Corneille said that Molière's troupe was magnificent! It is with reluctance that I must add that Corneille fell in love with Thérèse du Parc.

Very soon the company of Philibert du Croisy collapsed, as had that of Mitalla. Sieur du Croisy, a most pleasant man as well as a first-rate and versatile actor, made the correct choice. He came to Molière, who immediately invited him to join his troupe.

Playing at the Two Moors, and occasionally giving a benefit performance for the Rouen poorhouse, Molière completely captivated Rouen. However, without saying anything to anyone in the company, except, of course, Madeleine, he made three secret visits to Paris during that summer.

After his last visit, Molière finally revealed his plan to the

[82]

troupe. It transpired that, with the aid of certain favorable recommendations, he had managed to enter into contact with Court circles and had been presented to His Highness Philippe, Duc d'Orléans, the only brother of the reigning monarch Louis XIV.

The players listened to their director in utter silence.

Then Molière told them still more. He said that the King's only brother, having heard a great deal about the company, wished to extend it his patronage, and—possibly—allow it to use his name.

The hearts of the actors dropped, their hands trembled, their eyes lit up, and the word "Paris!" rolled through the Hall of Two Moors.

When the actors quieted down, Molière issued orders to load the theater's belongings and proceed to Paris.

The wagons approached the capital on an autumn evening in 1658. The sky was aflame with the October sunset. Leaves were falling in the nearby woods. And now the pointed roofs and rising cathedral spires came into view, so near that it seemed one could touch them with one's hand. And now the suburbs of the city were darkly visible.

Molière halted the caravan and stepped out of his carriage to stretch his legs. He walked a short distance away from the caravan and looked at the city which had driven him out twelve years earlier, ruined and disgraced. Fragmentary recollections flashed through his mind. For a moment he felt the stirrings of fear and the longing to turn back, to the warm Rhone; he heard the splashing of waves overboard, and the strumming strings of the Emperor of Entertainers. He felt old. It chilled him to think that he had nothing in his cart except his farces and his two comedies. He thought of the excellent Royal players at the Hôtel de Bourgogne, the great Scaramouche, his former teacher, who was performing in Paris, and the brilliant Paris ballet.

And he was tempted to return to Lyons and his old winter quarters. . . . And then, in summer—to the Mediterranean . . . He was suddenly frightened of the specter of the dank, vile prison which had almost swallowed him twelve years ago. And he whispered to himself, standing alone:

"Turn back? Yes, I will turn back. . . ."

He turned sharply, went to the head of the caravan, saw the faces of the actors and actresses looking out at him, and said to the front wagons:

"All right, let's go on!"

Chapter 11

Brou-ha-ha!

During the latter part of October, uncommon excitement reigned in the huge Salle des Gardes, also known as the Hall of the Caryatids, in the Old Louvre Palace. The air was filled with the screeching of saws, the deafening tattoo of hammers in the hands of theater builders. A stage was being constructed in the hall, then mounted with the necessary equipment. A machinist ran back and forth, mopping the sweat from his face, and the director's assistants hurried to and fro.

In the midst of all these, a homely, grimacing man, his caftan sleeves smudged with paint, was rushing about nervously, now shouting, now pleading with someone. His hands felt unpleasantly cold with excitement. Besides, he began to stutter, and this always terrified him. At times he snapped at the actors for no good reason, merely because it seemed to him that they were tangling underfoot and disturbing the workmen.

In the end everything was in due order, and on the

[85]

morning of October 24 the stage stood ready for the performance of Pierre Corneille's *Nicomède.*

It must be said that from the moment he entered Paris the director acted wisely, like a true, wily comedian. He arrived in the capital with his hat at a slant, and an ingratiating smile on his full lips. Who was helping him? Uninformed people thought that it was Prince Conti. But you and I know that the God-fearing Conti had nothing whatsoever to do with it. No! Molière was helped in his difficult path through the labyrinth of the Court by Pierre Mignard, the same Pierre Mignard whose heavy eyes had rested so discerningly upon him in Avignon. Mignard had enormous connections. It was chiefly thanks to him that Molière had gained entry to the all-powerful Cardinal Mazarin, and this was all that was needed to open a way to success.

The only thing that remained was to deal cleverly with Prince Philippe d'Orléans, the King's only brother.

And now, in the vast, gilded chamber, Molière, his head inclined, his left hand politely on the hilt of his sword, which is suspended from the widest band, is addressing His Highness:

"Oh, yes, much water has flowed under the bridge, Your Royal Highness, since my Illustre Théâtre perished at the White Cross. A naïve name, was it not? But alas, Your Highness, I assure you there was nothing illustrious in that theater! But then, Your Highness was only six years old at that time. Your Highness was a child. Your Highness is unrecognizable today!"

Philippe the French, Duc d'Orléans, also referred to as Monsieur, the King's only brother, an eighteen-year-old boy, stands, leaning on the massive table and listening politely to the entrepreneur. The two are studying one another.

The entrepreneur's face is set in a foxy smile; his whole face is a mask of honeyed lines, but his eyes are watchful and observant.

Philippe the French has the face of a youth, but already touched by secret passion. The boy looks at the director, his lips parted slightly. This mysterious man belongs to that strange world, the "actors' world." This man, so magnificently attired today, is said to have traveled in ox-drawn carts and to have slept in cattle sheds. Besides, everyone says that he can provide extraordinary entertainments.

Philippe the French examines his own response. It is ambivalent: one might think that he would be most impressed by the smile and the ingratiating folds on the actor's face, but certainly not by his eyes. Those eyes might even be described as somber. And Philippe wants to like the smile, but is drawn instead to the eyes. When the director began to speak, Philippe decided that his voice was unpleasant; besides, he drew his breath oddly as he spoke; people did not speak like that at the Court. But after the visitor's first sentences, he suddenly began to like his voice.

"Will Your Royal Highness permit me to present . . ."

Someone opens the heavy doors, and the visitor steps back, quite in accordance with etiquette, without turning his back to his host. Perhaps, after all, he has seen something of the world!

"Come in, ladies and gentlemen!" the visitor says, astonishing Philippe with the change in his voice, now stern and even harsh. And then, in the former voice, "Allow me to present to you"—and shifting again to the curt speech of people who travel by oxen—"Mademoiselle Madeleine Béjart, Mademoiselle du Parc, Mademoiselle de Brie . . ."

At the sight of the women, Philippe, imitating his brother, mechanically removes his plumed hat and listens. He sees the women and understands only that they are pale; they are of little interest to him. Then he sees the men and puts on his hat. And now somebody round as a ball, pug-nosed and smiling like the sun, is puffing heavily before him. It is Monsieur du Parc, from whom much can also be expected. Then someone else approaches, lame, with a smile on his lips, but pale with anxiety. And many others. Indeed, the visitor has a whole company.

Then everybody disappears, and Philippe d'Orléans says that he is most pleased, that he is very fond of the theater, that he has heard a great deal . . . He is pleased, he will take the company under his patronage . . . In fact, he is convinced that the King will not refuse to see how Monsieur de Molière's actors . . . Is he pronouncing the name correctly?

"Quite correctly, Your Royal Highness!"

Yes, he is certain that His Majesty will not refuse to see Monsieur de Molière's actors perform.

At these words, the visitor turns pale and says:

"Oh, Your Highness is too kind, but I shall try to justify your confidence . . ."

And in a third voice, somehow extraordinarily severe and impressive, the visitor asks and hopes that His Majesty is in good health, and also the Queen Mother.

And so it was, as a result of this interview, that the stage in the Salle des Gardes was set for *Nicomède.*

[88]

The man anxiously examines the sets, and again he is filled with apprehension and recalls the Rhone and the muscatel, and . . . There he had freedom, and none of this depressing responsibility. But it is late, it is too late to escape!

Is that a fire in the Old Louvre? No, these are thousands of candles burning in the chandeliers of the Hall of the Guards, and in their light the motionless caryatids come to life.

Monsieur de Molière, in the costume of Nicomède, looked numbly through an opening in the curtain as the hall filled up. It seemed to Monsieur de Molière that he was going blind. Diamonds flashed and glittered on every hand and sparkled on the sword-hilts. Before his eyes there was a forest of feathers, lace. His eyes were dazzled by the insignia on military jackets. Splendid ribbons shone on the gentlemen's chests, ornate coiffures waved over the ladies' heads.

The entire Court and its Guard were assembled in the hall.

And in front of all these, in an armchair, next to Philippe the French, sat a twenty-year-old man at the sight of whom the heart of the director of the troupe stopped altogether. This man—alone among the rest—was sitting there without removing his hat. In the haze of many breaths, Molière saw that the young man had a haughty face with unblinking eyes and a capriciously protruding lower lip.

But in the distance, Molière caught sight of faces which frightened him quite as much as the cold and arrogant face of the young man in the plumed hat. He discovered in the depth of the hall the familiar faces of the Royal players of the Bourgogne. "I knew it!" the director thought with an-

[89]

guish. "There they are, all of them." He recognized Madame Desoeillets, known for her ugliness and for her unrivaled greatness in tragic roles. Behind her face swam the faces of the men of the Bourgogne troupe—Montfleury, Beauchâteau, Raymond Poisson, Hauteroche, Villiers . . . The actors of the Royal troupe!

The first signal was given, and the director sprang away from the curtain. At the second signal, the hall became quiet, the curtain dropped, and from the stage came the words of Queen Laodicea, "Sir, I confess I am pleased to see . . ."

As *Nicomède* unfolded, the audience was more and more perplexed. First someone permitted himself to clear his throat, someone else coughed, then a third, and people of the theater know what a bad sign that is. Then they began to whisper and exchange astonished looks. What was this? For two weeks the name of Molière had flown back and forth throughout Paris, stirring the city and the Court! Molière this, and Molière that . . . Have you heard? From somewhere in the provinces . . . They say he is extraordinary! And he writes his own plays too? His Majesty will come to see him at the Salle des Gardes on the twenty-fourth. Have you been invited? Molière and Molière, nothing but Molière everywhere . . . And now, this? Corneille is played far better at the Bourgogne! Boredom became apparent in the faces of the courtiers. True, that du Parc is lovely. As for Molière himself . . . No, he is not bad, but how strangely he reads the verse—as though it were prose! Say what you will, the manner is odd!

But the eyes of one man in the audience, his face bloated with fat, expressed malicious joy rather than boredom. He was Zacharie Montfleury, one of the leading players at the Bourgogne. Villiers and Hauteroche whispered and gloated quietly nearby.

Nicomède came to a close, and was followed by a thin scattering of applause.

The young d'Orléans was mortified. He did not dare to raise his eyes and sat, sunk in his chair, his head drawn in between his shoulders.

At this moment, Monsieur de Molière, whose unfortunate passion for playing tragedies had put to the question his continued presence in Paris and the very future of French comedy, stepped out before the footlights. Small beads of sweat stood on his forehead. Molière bowed with a captivating smile. He opened his mouth. He wanted to say something.

Conversation in the hall died down.

And Monsieur de Molière said that, to begin with, he wished to express his gratitude to His and Her Majesties (Anne of Austria, the Queen Mother, was also in the hall) for their kindness and indulgence in overlooking obvious and inexcusable faults.

"That damned voice again," thought Philippe d'Orléans, who expected nothing more except vexation and disgrace. "It was the devil himself who brought them with their oxen to Paris, to humiliate me."

And Monsieur de Molière continued. No, he would venture beyond that: Their Majesties were magnanimous enough to overlook even presumption.

"May you be damned with your smiles!" thought d'Orléans.

But the smile did not impress the others unpleasantly. On the contrary, they seemed to like it.

[91]

And Monsieur de Molière went on, spinning his clever speech, saying that it was only his invincible desire to amuse Their Majesties that brought him there; he was entirely aware of the fact that he and his actors were merely pale copies, while the magnificent originals sat out there, in the hall . . .

At this point, many heads turned to look at the Bourgogne players.

"But perhaps Your Majesty will permit us to present a short farce? It is, of course, a mere trifle, undeserving of attention . . . But for some reason the provinces laughed! . . ."

The haughty young man in the plumed hat stirred for the first time, with an affirmative and courteous gesture.

And then, dripping with perspiration, the workmen and the actors hurriedly reset the stage behind the curtain for the farce *The Amorous Doctor,* composed by Monsieur de Molière himself during his sleepless nights on the road.

The solemn and proud heroes of Corneille's tragedy disappeared from the stage, giving way to Gorgibus, Gros-René, Sganarelle, and the rest of the personages of the farce. From the moment the amorous doctor, who could only with difficulty be recognized as the erstwhile Nicomède, ran out upon the stage, the audience began to smile. At his first grimace, they laughed. After his first words, they roared with laughter. Within a few moments, the laughter shook the walls. And even the haughty man in the armchair threw himself back and began to wipe his tears, sobbing with laughter. And suddenly, quite unexpectedly to himself, Philippe d'Orléans burst into high-pitched squeals.

The air turned bright before the eyes of the amorous

doctor. He was hearing familiar sounds. Making the usual pauses between his lines for the waves of laughter, he realized that he was hearing that inimitable, indescribable avalanche of laughter in the hall which testified to the fullest success of a comedy and which Molière's players called "brou-ha-ha!" The great comic actor felt a sweet chill creep up the back of his neck. "Victory!" he thought to himself. And he added more antics. And now even the musketeers who guarded the doors lost their reserve, and they, of all people, were not supposed to laugh under any circumstances.

The only members of the audience who did not laugh in the hall were the Bourgogne players, with the exception of Madame Desoeillets and one other person.

"Bring us through, Holy Virgin," prayed the doctor silently. "Here is another trick for you, and another, and another! Do your best, fat du Parc!"

"The devil! The devil take him! What a comic actor!" thought Montfleury in anguish. With fading eyes he looked around, and saw Villiers with bared teeth next to him. And beyond Villiers, with glittering eyes, the only man in the Bourgogne troupe who gave himself up to laughter without restraint or concern, a man in lace and ribbons, with a long sword at his thigh, the former officer of the Guards who had exchanged his long aristocratic name for the short stage name of Floridor. This man, with an aquiline nose and lean face, was a remarkable tragedian and the best Nicomède in France.

"But why the devil did he have to disgrace himself with *Nicomède* to start with?" wondered Floridor, doubling up with laughter. "Did he hope to compete with me? What for? We can easily share the stage between us: leave tragedy to me, and I'll give you comedy! What technique! Who can rival him? Unless it's Scaramouche? But even he . . ."

The finale of *The Amorous Doctor* was covered with such "brou-ha-ha" that the caryatids seemed to shake.

"Many thanks to d'Orléans, many thanks!" thought Zacharie Montfleury as the workmen pulled at the ropes and the curtain slid up, concealing the stage. "Brought us these devils from the provinces!"

The curtain fell, rose, and fell again. Then it rose and fell, rose and fell. Molière stood at the footlights, bowing, and the sweat dropped from his forehead onto the boards.

"Where is he from? . . . Who is he? . . . And all the rest of them? And that fat du Parc? . . . And the maidservant? . . . Who taught them? . . . Gentlemen, they are better than the Italians! The grimaces of that Molière, Your Majesty . . ."

"I told you, Your Majesty," Philippe d'Orléans said to Louis sedately. But the latter did not listen to his brother. He was still wiping his eyes, as though crying for the loss of someone near and dear.

Ah, dear, dead grandfather Cressé! What a pity you were not at the Hall of the Guards on October 24, 1658!

It was decreed that the Players of His Highness Duc d'Orléans, Philippe the French, be given a hall at the Petit Bourbon and confirmed in the pension declared by the Duc d'Orléans. They were to take turns with the Italian troupe, one day for the Italians, one for the French. And so be it!

Chapter 12
Petit Bourbon

Anagram: Élomire-Molière

To the astonishment of everyone
There's Élomire in the Petit Bourbon.
—LE BOULANGER DE CHALUSSAY,
Élomire the Hypochondriac, 1670

According to the Royal edict, Monsieur de Molière moved
his theater to the Petit Bourbon palace, to share it amicably
with the Italian troupe. *The Amorous Doctor* pleased the
King so well that he ordered a subsidy of fifteen hundred
livres to be paid Molière's company annually, on condition
that Molière recompense the Italians for invading their theater. And Molière agreed to pay the Italians, headed by his
old teacher Scaramouche, exactly the sum he was to receive
from the King.

Molière's company was granted the name of The Players
of Monsieur, the King's Only Brother, and the latter immediately decreed the payment of three hundred livres annually to each member of his troupe. Alas, it must be admitted

here that not one of those three hundred livres was ever paid, perhaps because the treasury of the King's brother was in such a sorry state.

"In any event, the intentions of His Highness were of the noblest," the actors would remark sadly.

It was decided that all income would be divided among the players according to their shares, while Molière would, in addition, receive the author's fees for his plays.

The days of the performances were easily divided with the Italians. Molière was to play on Mondays, Tuesdays, Thursdays, and Saturdays. Later, when the Italians left, Molière played on Sundays, Tuesdays, and Fridays.

The Petit Bourbon palace stood between the church of Saint Germain l'Auxerrois and the Old Louvre. Over the main entrance to the Petit Bourbon the word "Hope" was inscribed in large letters, but the palace itself and all the coats of arms and decorations in it were chipped and broken, for the recent internecine war had left its mark on it too. Within the palace there was a rather large theater with galleries along the side walls, and doric columns with loges between them. The ceiling in the theater was decorated with painted fleurs-de-lys; cross-shaped chandeliers hung above the stage, and metal sconces were attached along the walls of the hall.

The hall had a long history. In 1614 it had been the scene of the last sessions of the États Général (not counting those assembled one hundred and seventy-five years later by Louis XVI). It was in this hall that the elder of the Paris Merchants Guild, the president of the Third Estate, had pleaded with the King to save "the poor people, who were left with nothing but skin and bones." And beginning with 1615, when the Royal ballet had danced there, the hall had been used for theatrical performances, chiefly by Italian companies. But Frenchmen played there as well. The theatrical life of the Petit Bourbon was interrupted only during the Fronde, when it was used as a prison for state criminals charged with offenses against His Majesty. And it was they who had mutilated the decorations.

After the end of the Fronde, Pierre Corneille's *Andromède* was produced in the hall, with elaborate sets and musical accompaniment. The music, incidentally, had been the work of our old acquaintance d'Assouci, who later insisted that it was he who had given soul to Corneille's verse.

Finally, the hall was assigned to the Italians, who were much beloved in Paris. Not only were they excellent players, but their first-rate machinist and artist, Torelli, had equipped the stage with such remarkable mechanisms that the Italians could perform wonders in their fantastic entertainments.

Jean Loret, a theatrical feuilletonist of that time, expressed his admiration for the Italian equipment in bad verse:

> Flying wildly through the air
> Fearful devils people scare.
> You may go from France to China—
> Nothing like it anywhere.

In addition to their mechanical devices, the Italians also had a magnificent ballet company, as noted by the same Loret:

> There is no greater pleasure—
> Whatever you may say—
> Than seeing the magnificent
> Italian ballet.

[97]

And it was in the neighborhood of this extraordinary troupe that Molière and his players were now installed.

When he first came to Paris in October, Jean-Baptiste went to his father's house and tenderly embraced him. The old man could not quite understand the astonishing success of his elder son, who had renounced his title and abandoned his trade to devote himself to the art of the comedian. But his glittering sword, costly clothing, and the fact that Jean-Baptiste had become the director of the King's brother's troupe overwhelmed the old man and reconciled him to his son.

After restoring his strength with bouillon and a rest in his father's house following the ordeals of October 24, Molière began to organize his life in Paris and started rehearsals at the Petit Bourbon.

On November 2, 1658, Molière opened his performances at the Petit Bourbon—again not with a comedy, but with Corneille's tragedy *Héraclius.* The acting was tolerably good, and there was a fair-sized audience; nevertheless, Paris was nonplussed. Some people asserted that the company "of that . . . what do you call him . . . Molière" played remarkably well, demonstrating how the King laughed. Those were the people who had seen *The Amorous Doctor* at the Salle des Gardes. Others said that the company's acting was very mediocre, and could not understand all the fanfare with which Molière had been given the Petit Bourbon. Those were the spectators who had seen *Héraclius.*

There was a good deal of disputation, and it ended in a run on the Petit Bourbon. Everyone wanted to see for himself what this newcomer Molière represented. This wave of spectators witnessed *Nicomède* and *The Amorous Doctor,* and Paris was flooded with a new party of enthusiasts. However, they said little about *Nicomède,* merely extolling the beauty of Mademoiselle du Parc and shouting that "this Molière" was unutterably funny and that his farce was superb.

The next groups of theatergoers were not as lucky. Molière put on three Corneille plays in succession: *Rodogune, The Death of Pompey,* and *The Cid.* At this point the audiences rebelled and, most fortunately, a certain choleric Parisian who stood in the pit during the rather boring performance of *Pompey* threw an apple at the head of Monsieur de Molière, who was impersonating Caesar. This piece of impertinence cleared the director's head and he announced *The Bungler.* The situation immediately reversed itself: success was complete.

And here we must, after all, take another look at the reason for Molière's fiascos in tragedies. Was it that the Bourgogne troupe played very well, or that Molière played badly? The answer is: neither one nor the other. To begin with, Molière played tragedies in a style entirely different from the familiar one of that time. The Bourgogne troupe had great actors like Madame Desoeillets and Monsieur Floridor, but it also had mediocre and weak performers. All of them were followers of the same Bellerose whom Grandfather Cressé had admired so wholeheartedly, but who had elicited the following comment from a certain Parisian of excellent taste:

"The devil take him! When he plays, you feel that he does not understand a single word of what he is saying!"

[99]

Of course, this comment is somewhat exaggerated. Yet it must be admitted that Bellerose's acting was false, it did not convey a sense of living inner experience.

The obese and pathologically envious Zacharie Montfleury enjoyed enormous popularity in Paris. However, the Epicurean Cyrano de Bergerac said of him:

"Montfleury imagines that he is a great figure simply because it is impossible to thrash him all over with sticks in a single day."

Generally, that witty and subtle connoisseur of the stage Bergerac hated Montfleury so violently that he permitted himself one day, in a drunken state, to cause a row in the theater, showering Montfleury with abuse and driving him off the stage. And what does this show? It shows, first, that the conduct of Monsieur de Bergerac, playwright and disciple of Gassendi, was occasionally disgraceful: a player at that time was an easy object of attack, and there was no particular valor in insulting him. But it also shows that to innovators of fine taste the old-fashioned manner of singsong declamation was intolerable. And this was the manner of all the Bourgogne players, good and bad.

But Molière had from his very first steps on the stage, even in his l'Illustre Théâtre, attempted to create a school of natural and inwardly convincing rendition of the dramatic text. This was the manner in which Molière himself began and which he taught his players.

What was wrong, then? It would seem that Molière should have been victorious and that his system of acting should have won the hearts of his audiences. Unfortunately, it was not so. Molière applied his system primarily to tragedy, for which he had neither the temperament nor the voice. Hence, he knew very well how tragedy should be played, but he played it badly. As regards his colleagues, many of them possessed the requisite qualities for playing tragedy, but Molière's system was still too new to win over the audiences at once.

And, of course, when the Bourgogne players, who possessed excellently trained voices, sang out the closing lines of their pseudo-classical monologues (and Montfleury was particularly skillful in this), they won overwhelming applause. The Parisians of that time wanted to see mighty heroes in coats of armor, heroes who delivered thunderous tirades, and not people as simple and modest as they themselves were in daily life. This was the reason for the failure of Molière's tragic productions.

The Bungler was followed at the Petit Bourbon by *The Amorous Quarrel,* with equally great success. Philibert du Croisy, who had joined the company, contributed substantially to this success with his performance in the role of the ridiculous scholar Metaphrastus.

After *The Amorous Quarrel,* the Italian troupe began to feel the danger of the presence of its neighbor, the Frenchman Molière. The Paris audience, accustomed to attending only the Italian days at the Petit Bourbon, now came in droves on Molière's days as well. Gold coins flowed into the cash box of the former itinerant players who were now the Players of the Duc d'Orléans. The actors' shares increased, and Paris buzzed with talk of Molière.

But what was it that was said about him, to begin with? First, people began to say that the playwright Molière was shamelessly using the works of Italian writers and imitating them. In time, it became so fashionable to accuse Molière of plagiarism that, when it was impossible to point out what he had stolen and where, people said that he had "evidently" stolen. But when there was no ground even for such a charge, it was said that he "might have" imitated this or that . . . In the end, people attributed to Molière the boastful phrase "I take my goods wherever I find them!" although he had never said anything of the sort. What he said was altogether different. He said, "I am recovering my goods," hinting at the plagiarisms committed at his expense.

In reality, Molière, who had an excellent knowledge not only of classical, but also of Italian and Spanish drama, often borrowed plots from his predecessors, occasionally adopting certain characters or even entire scenes. Should this strange procedure be condemned? I don't know. But I can say that, according to general comments, everything borrowed by Molière turned out in his version immeasurably superior to the original models. It was especially after *The Amorous Quarrel* that critics wrote that the basic contents of this play were derived from the comedy *Cupidity,* written some seventy-five years earlier by the Italian Niccolò Secchi. He might also have borrowed from another Italian play, *Amorous Misadventures,* or utilized an idea expressed in one of the works of the classic author Horace. He might, finally, have borrowed a few things from *The Gardener's Dog,* by the most famous of Spanish playwrights, Lope Felix de Vega Carpio, who died when Molière sat as a boy in his father's shop. As for Lope de Vega, it would have been easy enough to borrow from him, for he had written some eighteen hundred plays and had been nicknamed with good reason the Phoenix of Spain and a Wonder of Nature.

In short, as you see, my hero had read a good deal, including Spanish works.

And so, *The Amorous Quarrel,* based on a borrowed plot, won enormous success and played to the enthusiastic applause of the Parisian audience, evoking the close and hostile attention of the Bourgogne theater.

The year 1659 was marked by many events, related chiefly to changes in the troupe. At Easter time, a young man called Charles Varlet La Grange presented himself respectfully to Molière and asked permission to join the company. The specialty of the young man, whose strong and earnest face was adorned by a small pointed mustache, was that of the romantic lead. Molière liked him at once and accepted him into the troupe. And, in the view of those who have studied the life of my hero for several centuries, this was a most fortunate action.

During his very first days with the troupe, Sieur de La Grange obtained a thick notebook, which he named "The Register," and began a daily record of everything that occurred in Moliére's company. Sieur de La Grange noted the deaths and the marriages of actors, their departures from the troupe, the arrival of new ones, the number of performances and their names, the moneys received, and so forth. Without this precious "Register" kept by La Grange and decorated with his symbolic sketches, we would know still less about our hero than we know today, or, to put it more precisely, we would know virtually nothing.

And so, La Grange joined the company, but Dufresne left the capital to return to his native Normandy. The Marais theater invited the du Parcs to join it, and they left the Molière troupe after some clash with the director. This was a serious loss. It was somewhat balanced by the addition to the troupe of the most famous comedian of the Marais and the Bourgogne, Julien Bedeau, who played under the name of Jodelet, after the comic character of Scarron's plays. He was an excellent acquisition. Unfortunately, not for long: he died the following year. Together with Jodelet came his brother, Sieur de l'Espy, who had also left the Marais. He played the funny old men usually called Gorgibus.

And, finally, we must record the sad event of May, 1659: one of the original members of the troupe and the Children of the Family, the lover Joseph Béjart, who stuttered to the end of his days, left the company. The entire troupe escorted him to the cemetery, and the theater was in mourning for several days.

Thus the year 1659 passed in feverish work, in bustling activities and excitements, in a succession of triumphs and vexations, and its end was marked by a notable event.

Chapter 13

Lampoon on the Blue Salon

MAROTTE: A valet here is asking if you are at home. He says his master wants to come and see you.

MAGDELON: Fool! Learn to express yourself less vulgularly. Say: "A servitor begs to inquire whether it is convenient for you to receive!"

—The Precious Ladies Ridiculed

If you were to ask any fashionable Parisian of the first half of the seventeenth century which was the most pleasant place in Paris, he would reply without hesitation, "The blue salon of Madame de Rambouillet."

Daughter of the French ambassador to Rome, born de Vivonne, the Marquise de Rambouillet was an exquisitely refined lady. Her refinement dated back to her earliest childhood (there are such natures!). Having married and settled in Paris, the Marquise decided, not without good reason, that Paris society was somewhat crude. She therefore resolved to surround herself with the best that could be found in the capital, and began to assemble in her house the flower of society. She furnished and decorated a number of rooms for her receptions, but the most famous of these was her salon in which everything was upholstered in light blue velvet.

Madame de Rambouillet's greatest interest was in literature, and her salon therefore became chiefly literary. But, on the whole, the company that flocked to the salon was quite diverse. There was Jean-Louis Balzac, society writer, glittering in his armchair. There was the disenchanted thinker the Duc de La Rochefoucauld, who mournfully attempted to persuade Madame de Rambouillet that our virtues are nothing but hidden vices. When the assembled guests were thoroughly depressed by the arguments of the gloomy Duke, their gaiety was restored by the vivacious wit Vincent Voiture. And most fascinating disputations were conducted by the Messieurs Cotin, Chapelain, Gilles Ménage, and many others.

As soon as it became known that the best minds of Paris were gathering at the Hotel de Rambouillet, the salon was invaded by a number of most charming marquises with lace at their knees, by evening wits, frequenters of theatrical premieres, and authors of amorous madrigals and tender sonnets. These were followed by worldly abbés and, naturally, by a bevy of ladies.

Among the guests of the salon there was also Bossuet, who subsequently made himself famous by delivering moving funeral orations at the graveside of virtually every defunct Frenchman of any consequence. Indeed, his very first sermon was delivered (this time, not over a departed celebrity) at Madame Rambouillet's salon when he was only sixteen years old.

Bossuet declaimed until late into the night, which provided Voiture with an opportunity to comment when the orator had finally discharged himself of every idea he had accumulated in his mind:

"Sir, I have never before heard anyone deliver a sermon at so early an age and so late an hour."

The ladies who frequented the salon very soon introduced the custom of calling one another "my precious" as they exchanged kisses in greeting. The expression "precious" gained much favor in Paris, and remained as a permanent designation for the ladies who adorned the Rambouillet gatherings.

The scene resounded with verses in honor of the precious Marquise, whom the poets called "the enchanting Arthénice," transposing the letters of her name, Catherine. In honor of her young daughter, Julie Rambouillet, who glittered in her mother's salon, the poets composed entire wreaths of madrigals. These madrigals were followed by witticisms, fabricated principally by the marquises. Their witticisms were so elaborate that they required lengthy explanations. There were, however, some rejected individuals outside the walls of the salon who asserted that those witticisms were simply stupid, and their authors utterly devoid of talent.

But all of this would not have been so bad had Catherine de Rambouillet and her suite not turned their attention from madrigals and witticisms to major literature. New works were read aloud and discussed in the blue salon. Opinions were formed, and these opinions became mandatory in Paris.

As time went on, the level of the refinement rose, the ideas voiced at the salon became increasingly cryptic, and the forms in which they were invested more and more ornate.

A simple mirror in which the precious ladies examined their reflections became, in their language, "the counselor of grace." In reply to some pleasantry uttered by a marquis, a lady would say:

"Marquis, you are adding the wood of flattery to the fire in the hearth of friendship."

A certain lady, the sister of the playwright Georges de Scudéry, became the virtual lawgiver in the Rambouillet salon, as well as in others started in their homes by imitators of Madame de Rambouillet. Georges de Scudéry won his renown, to begin with, by regarding himself as not simply a playwright, but the leading playwright in France. Secondly, he was noted for the absolute lack of any dramatic talent. Thirdly, he created a furore by attacking Corneille's greatest play, *The Cid,* immediately on its appearance, doing his utmost to prove that the play was immoral and, besides, that it was not a play at all, since it violated the Aristotelian laws governing drama, lacking unity of place, time, and action. True enough, Scudéry never succeeded in convincing anyone; no one can ever prove, even with Aristotle's aid, that a work which is successful, which is written in excellent verse, which has an interesting plot and effective, sharply delineated parts, is not a play. And it's not for nothing that my hero—upstart, Royal Valet and Upholsterer —was wont to say in later years that all those Aristotelian rules were sheer nonsense, and that there was only one rule: plays should be written with skill and talent.

Well, then, the envious Georges de Scudéry had a sister, Madeleine. At first she had been a guest at the Rambouillet salon, but later she founded a salon of her own, and at a ripe age composed a novel she titled *Clélie, A Roman Story*. Properly speaking, Rome had nothing to do with the story at all. Under the guise of Romans, the novel depicted eminent Parisians. The novel was elegant, false, and pompous in the extreme. The novel was enormously popular among the Parisians, and to the ladies it became virtually a bible, especially since the first volume included so delectable an appendix as an allegorical Map of Tenderness, containing a River of Propensity, a Lake of Indifference, a village called Love Letters, and so on in the same vein.

A wagonload of nonsense had invaded French literature, and the trash had completely enslaved the precious heads. In addition, the admirers of Madeleine de Scudéry had utterly corrupted the language and even threatened to subvert the orthography. One of these ladies had hatched a remarkable plan: in order to make orthography accessible to women, who were, as usual, lagging considerably behind the men in mastering its intricacies, the lady proposed that words be written as they were pronounced. But before the lips that opened to discuss this project had time to close, disaster struck the precious ladies.

In November, 1659, a rumor spread abroad that Monsieur de Molière was about to produce a new one-act comedy at the Petit Bourbon. Its title intrigued the public: the play was called *The Precious Ladies Ridiculed*. On October 18, together with Corneille's *Cinna*, Molière presented his new play.

Its very first words electrified the audience. During the fifth scene (according to the text that survives today) the ladies' eyes bulged. The eighth scene struck at the marquises who sat, as was the custom at the time, along the sides of the stage. And the parterre burst into laughter and laughed until the end of the play.

The contents of the play were as follows: two silly damsels, Cathos and Magdelon, who had stuffed their heads with Scudéry, rejected their suitors because they were not, by the ladies' standards, sufficiently refined. The suitors avenged themselves upon the precious ladies. They dressed up their valets as marquises, and these impostors paid the silly girls a visit. The girls received the two rogues with open arms. The impudent Mascarille held the ladies spellbound with preposterous tales, and the other impostor, Jodelet, enchanted them with lies about his military career. Mascarille, a brazen-faced scoundrel, not only declaimed, but even sang a poem of his own composition, which went approximately as follows:

> While in a heedless moment brief,
> Oh, oh! I gazed at you today,
> Your eye had slyly spirited my heart away.
> Stop thief, stop thief, stop thief, stop thief!

"Stop thief, stop thief," howled the valet to the roaring of the parterre.

Everything had been demolished by ridicule: the Maps of Tenderness, the salons in which such verses were read, the authors of these verses, and the guests of the salons. And yet it was impossible for the latter to protest, since the comedy involved only valets disguised as marquises rather than real marquises.

The farce presented on the stage was riotous and by no means innocent. It mocked the manners and customs of

[110]

contemporary Paris, while the originators of these customs were right there, in the loges and on the stage. The parterre roared with laughter and pointed its fingers at them. It recognized the gentry of the salons, whom the former upholsterer held up to scorn in the eyes of all. Anxious whispers were exchanged in the loges. A rumor spread instantly throughout the hall that Cathos was unquestionably Catherine de Rambouillet, and Magdelon, Madeleine de Scudéry.

The marquises sitting on the stage turned purple. The bearers brought in Mascarille-Molière. His idiotic peruke was so huge that its ends swept the floor as he bowed, and it was topped by a hat as tiny as a fist. A monstrous mass of lace adorned his breeches at the knees. The would-be marquis Jodelet was played by old Jodelet. And the two comedians Molière and Jodelet did everything but walk on their heads to amuse the public, indulging in a series of ambiguous and most suggestive antics. The other performers, including Mademoiselle de Brie, who played Magdelon, the daughter of Gorgibus, held up their ends with appropriate zest.

Just look, the comedy seemed to say, at our charming marquises and our precious young ladies! But, pardon me, these are only lackeys? They are lackeys, certainly, but from whom did they take over such manners? Everything was mocked, ridiculed, held up to derision! The dress, to its last ribbon, the verses, the pomposity, the falseness, the rudeness toward inferiors!

When Molière glanced at the public through the slits in his mask he caught sight of the esteemed Madame de Rambouillet sitting in front of her stall with her suite behind her. The precious old lady, as everyone had noticed, was green with rage. She had clearly grasped the import of the play. Nor was she aione in this! An old man in the parterre called out in the midst of the action:

"Bravo, Molière! This is real comedy!"

The bolt had struck so near the ranks of the precious ones themselves that they were thrown into immediate panic. The first to abandon Madame de Rambouillet's army was one of her staunchest admirers and banner-bearers, who threw the banner entrusted to him straight into the mud. This deserter was none other than the poet Monsieur de Ménage.

Leaving the theater after the performance, Ménage took Monsieur Chapelain under the arm and whispered:

"My dear, we shall have to burn the idols we adored. . . . I must confess, we indulged in a good deal of nonsense in the salons!"

To this, Ménage added that the play, in his opinion, was caustic and effective, and that, generally, he had foreseen all this. . . .

But what Ménage had foreseen we do not know, since his subsequent words were lost in the clatter of the carriages before the theater.

The lights in the hall went out. The streets were now completely dark. Molière, wrapped in his cloak, with a lantern in his hand, hurried to Madeleine's, coughing a little in the November damp. He was drawn by the fire in the hearth, but even more by something else. He hurried to see Madeleine's sister and ward, Armande Béjart, the same Menou who had played Éphyre in Lyons six years before. She was now a young lady of sixteen. Molière hurried to see Armande, but he cringed painfully at the thought of

Madeleine's eyes. Those eyes became unpleasant every time Molière would enter into a lively exchange with the vivacious and coquettish Armande.

Madeleine had forgiven everything. She had forgiven the Lyons incident with du Parc; she had forgiven and made peace with Madame de Brie. But now it was as though a demon had taken possession of her.

A lantern is speeding along the embankment through the dank fog of the November night. Monsieur de Molière! Tell us, whisper it, no one can hear us now, how old are you? Thirty-eight, and she is sixteen? Besides, who are her father and her mother? Are you certain that she is Madeleine's sister?

He does not want to answer. It may well be that he does not know. Why, then, waste words on the subject? We might talk of something else. Of the mistake, for example, which Molière had committed in his *The Precious Ladies* when he shot a dart at the Bourgogne players:

"Which actors will you give your play to?"

"The King's Players, naturally," the scoundrel Mascarille replies caustically. "They are the only ones who know how to recite verse!"

Monsieur de Molière should not have struck out at the Bourgogne. To discerning people it is clear that he is a man of another school and is creating this school, while Montfleury is by no means as bad an actor as Bergerac asserted. The paths of the Bourgogne and of Molière are different, and the Bourgogne should not be attacked, especially since such thrusts do not prove anything, and it is dangerous to offend everyone!

[113]

Chapter 14

He Who Sows the Wind

On the very next day Monsieur de Molière received official notice from the Paris authorities, banning all further performances of *The Precious Ladies Ridiculed*.

"Hangmen!" Monsieur de Molière muttered, lowering himself into an armchair. "Who could have done it?"

Yes, indeed, who could have done it? No one knows. It was said that the ban had been obtained by some eminent and influential habitué of salons of the type of Madame de Rambouillet's. In any event, we must give the precious ones their just due: they answered Molière's blow with their own powerful one.

When he recovered some of his composure, Molière began to think of what could be done and where he might turn to save the play. There was but a single person in France who could save the situation. He alone could protect Molière in this nasty situation. But, alas, as if in spite, this person was away from Paris at the time.

Then my hero decided, first of all, to send his play to this person for examination. And he immediately drew up a letter in his mind, defending the play:

"Your Majesty! This is an obvious misunderstanding! *The Precious Ladies* is nothing but a gay comedy. Your Majesty, with your exceptional taste and subtle discernment, will unquestionably permit the performance of this amusing trifle!"

The play was sent to the King. In addition, the enterprising director of the Petit Bourbon undertook a series of other actions. There was a conference with Madeleine; the alarmed troupe ran this way and that; Molière went somewhere to make inquiries and to bow; and, on returning, he decided to resort to yet another method of bringing his play back to life.

This method has long been familiar to playwrights: under powerful pressure, the author deliberately mutilates his work. It is an extreme method! Thus a lizard, caught by its tail, breaks off the tail and escapes. For every lizard realizes that it is better to live without a tail than to lose its life altogether.

Molière felt, with good reason, that the King's censors did not know that changes in the work could not alter its essential meaning a single iota or weaken its undesirable impact upon the viewer.

What Molière broke off was not the tail, but the beginning of the play, deleting an opening scene; he also went over other places in the play, spoiling them as best he could. The opening scene was necessary, and its removal weakened the play, but changed nothing in its central theme. This scene had evidently indicated that Cathos and Magdelon were Parisiennes, and the author's aim was to reassure the

[115]

censors by stressing that the two young ladies were provincials who had recently come to Paris.

While the cunning comedian was slyly mutilating his play, all Paris was agog. The only topic of conversation both in the city and for dozens of *lieues* around it was *The Precious Ladies Ridiculed*. Fame knocked at Monsieur de Molière's door, taking the shape, in the first place, of a certain literary gentleman named Somaize. The latter stormed in the salons, trying to prove that Molière was simply a plagiarist, in addition to being an empty and superficial farceur. And others agreed with him.

"He stole it all from Abbé de Pure!" some writers were shouting in the salons.

"No, no!" argued others. "The plot and characters of this farce were stolen from the Italians!"

News of the ban added oil to the flames. Everybody wanted to see the play which ridiculed people of the highest circles, habitués of salons. While the Parisians were excitedly discussing the news, a bookseller, Guillaume de Luynes, came to the theater and humbly requested a copy of the play, which request was denied. In short, everyone was striving in his own direction, and ultimately, Molière's wily machinations brought results.

He found patrons among the powerful, cleverly hinted that he would seek the protection of the King, and two weeks later the comedy was admitted to performance, but with revisions.

The company was jubilant, and Madeleine whispered a single phrase into Molière's ear:

"Double the admission!"

[116]

The practical Madeleine was right. The theater's unerring barometer—the box office—indicated storm. The second performance was given on December 2, and that evening the theater, which usually took in approximately four hundred livres an evening, brought in one thousand and four hundred livres. And this continued. Molière began to present *The Precious Ladies* in combination with Corneille or Scarron plays, and each time to full houses.

The feuilletonist Jean Loret, wrote in his verse *Gazette* that the play was trivial and cheap, but admittedly very funny:

> I thought I'd surely split my sides
> With laughter loud and jolly!
> For thirty sous—admission price—
> I laughed for ten pistole!

The bookseller and publisher de Luynes finally achieved his goal. In some mysterious manner he managed to obtain a copy of the manuscript of *The Precious Ladies,* and he informed Molière that he was about to publish the play. The latter had no choice but to agree. He wrote an introduction, which opened with the words: "It is strange indeed that people are published against their will!" In reality, of course, there was nothing unpleasant in the fact that the play was being published, especially since the introduction gave the author an opportunity to express some of his ideas concerning *The Precious Ladies.*

The precious ones, said Molière, need not take offense at the play, for it depicted merely their ridiculous imitators. Everything good in this world usually provokes foolish aping. And so on in the same vein. Besides, Molière modestly asserted that he had stayed within the bounds of honest and permitted satire in composing the play.

It is not likely that Molière convinced anyone with his introduction. There were people in Paris who commented that satire, as every literate person knew, could indeed be honest. But they doubted that there was a single man in the world who could submit to the authorities a sample of permissible satire. However, we must leave it to Molière to defend himself as best he can. This is essential for him, for, quite obviously, he had drawn to himself a good deal of close attention since the premiere of *The Precious Ladies*. And, whether he wanted it or not, he continued to write in a manner which made sure that this attention did not slacken.

Chapter 15

The Puzzling Monsieur Ratabon

It soon became clear that Molière was, as the saying goes, a playwright by the grace of God. He worked rapidly and had an easy command of verse. While he was being denounced by the Paris literati and the actors of the Hôtel de Bourgogne, he wrote a new comedy in verse, *Sganarelle, or the Imaginary Cuckold*. It was ready by spring and was presented on May 28, 1660, with the participation of the du Parcs, who had returned to Molière after a brief stay at the Marais, the de Bries, L'Espy, Madeleine, and Molière.

The season was dull, since the King was away from Paris, and hence many of the nobles were also absent. Nevertheless, the play attracted keen attention, especially in view of the scandal that broke out at the very first performance.

A certain bourgeois raised a great outcry in the hall, declaring that Monsieur de Molière had put him to public ridicule by portraying him as Sganarelle. Naturally, his outburst delighted the audience. The wags made merry as they listened to the raging bourgeois, who threatened to lodge a complaint with the police against the comedian who was

[119]

making sport of the family life of honest folk. This was, of course, a sheer misunderstanding. Molière had not thought of any individual bourgeois as he was writing *The Imaginary Cuckold*. He had merely drawn a general portrait of a jealous husband and avaricious man. We suspect that many people recognized themselves in Sganarelle, but were cleverer than the gentleman who shouted in the hall, and kept the knowledge to themselves.

Thus, after gaining several dozen enemies among the Paris literary circles thanks to *The Precious Ladies,* Molière proceeded to pick a quarrel with the good bourgeois from the commercial districts as well.

The Imaginary Cuckold was heatedly discussed in the Paris salons, the views expressed by the literary gentry being fairly uniform:

"A trifling piece! A crude little contrivance, built on comic situations and vulgar jests."

They sought to discover where Molière had stolen his plot, but their researches were not crowned with particular success.

After several performances, Molière found a letter in his dressing room. A certain Neuf-Villenaine wrote that, having seen his comedy *The Imaginary Cuckold,* he found it so excellent that one viewing was not sufficient, and he had seen it six times. Such a beginning made Molière flush with pleasure, for he had lately begun to observe with astonishment that fame was quite different from what many people imagined it to be, expressing itself, as it did, chiefly in unrestrained abuse on every street corner.

He went on reading the flattering letter. As he read on, he found that Monsieur Neuf-Villenaine possessed a truly phenomenal memory: after six visits to the theater, he had the full text of the comedy written down. At this point Monsieur de Molière sensed danger, and no wonder, for Monsieur Neuf-Villenaine informed him that he had composed his own commentaries on every scene of *The Imaginary Cuckold*. And now, with these commentaries, he was about to have the play published, for, as he put it "this is absolutely essential for the sake of your fame and mine!"

"Dishonorable persons" went on Monsieur Neuf-Villenaine, "may publish poorly verified versions of the play, and thus inflict damage upon Monsieur de Molière."

In short, Monsieur Neuf-Villenaine was sending the play to the publisher Jean Ribou, on the Quai des Grands-Augustins.

"I swear," cried Molière as he finished reading the letter from the fame-loving Monsieur Neuf-Villenaine, "there isn't a more brazen scoundrel in the world!"

As to that last comment, Monsieur de Molière was, perhaps, somewhat mistaken!

The summer of 1660 was marked by the fact that Molière finally had the opportunity, breaking away from the current repertory at the Petit Bourbon, to present *The Precious Ladies* before the King. On July 29 the play was performed at the Vincennes woods near Paris, where the young King had gone for a rest in the lap of nature. The play enjoyed complete success. And now it became entirely evident that Louis XIV entertained a great love of the theater, and particularly of comedy, which the experienced director of Le Petit Bourbon took into immediate account.

Afterward the troupe returned to Paris and continued with its repertory, which was beginning to indicate beyond doubt that Molière's plays outdid all others, in both the comic and the tragic veins, in the number of performances and the box office returns.

On August 30 Molière presented *The Precious Ladies* befor the King's only brother and his suite at the Louvre, again with enormous success. The itinerant comedian's sun was clearly rising. The greatest of careers seemed to await the company, and it began the autumn season of 1660 with pleasant anticipations of successes to come. But in October, four days after the death of the poor satirist Scarron, who had finally found surcease in the grave after the bitter sufferings resulting from a stroke, a sudden misfortune broke over the heads of the troupe. The director of the Company of the King's Brother, which had enjoyed unclouded success at court, was expelled from the Petit Bourbon with all his players.

On a dripping Monday, October 11, Monsieur Ratabon, chief superintendent of all the Royal buildings, appeared in the Petit Bourbon. He was mysteriously preoccupied with something, and was accompanied by an architect with drawings and plans in his hands. The architect was followed by a crowd of workmen carrying pickaxes, shovels, crowbars, and hatchets. The worried actors questioned Monsieur Ratabon as to the meaning of this visit, to which Ratabon drily and civilly declared that he had come to wreck the Petit Bourbon.

"But why?" cried the actors. "And where shall we play?"

Monsieur Ratabon civilly replied that he did not know anything about that.

When Molière appeared, the entire situation was instantly clarified: Ratabon had come with a magnificent and fully detailed plan for the rebuilding of the Louvre, which required not only that the Petit Bourbon, but also the church of Saint-Germain-l'Auxerrois which adjoined it, be razed to the ground.

The floor rocked under Molière's feet.

"So we're being thrown out into the street without warning?" he asked.

Ratabon merely shrugged with sympathy. Formally, he was entirely in his right: it was in no way a part of his duties to notify the director of the players concerning the Royal Architect's plans for reconstructions of the King's buildings.

And so the axes went to work at once, and plaster dust filled the air.

When he recovered from the initial shock, Molière rushed to seek protection from the patron of the company—the King's brother. And the King's brother . . .

But let us first return for a moment to Monsieur Ratabon. What, indeed, could have been his reasons for starting the demolition of the theater without a single word of warning to the Court players? It surely cannot be assumed that Monsieur Ratabon had absent-mindedly failed to notice the actors playing in his immediate neighborhood—and not one company, but two, although at this time the Italian troupe was no longer in Paris, having left France. We must therefore conclude that Superintendent Ratabon had deliberately refrained from informing the company of the imminent demolition of its theater.

Even worse, he concealed all the preparations for this action, to make sure that the company would have no time to take steps to save itself. If this was so (and it was precisely so), then we may well ask: what prompted Super-intendent Ratabon to such conduct?

Alas! There can be only one explanation. Namely, that Ratabon was the instrument of a powerful group of enemies who had conceived a hatred for Molière and his work from his very first days in Paris. It was even rumored that the superintendent had been bribed. But the identities of those who directed his hand are not known.

Well, then, the King's brother took the liveliest interest in the fate of the company, and the situation at the Petit Bourbon was immediately reported to the King. The super-intendent was summoned before His Majesty, and offered a brief but full explanation of the facts, submitting the plans for the future colonnades and buildings for His Majesty's consideration.

What, then, was to be done with the troupe of the Duc d'Orléans, which found itself in the street? The young King instantly solved the problem. Did the King of France have only one theater building in Paris? The company of Monsieur de Molière was to be installed at the Palais Royal, formerly called the Palais Cardinal.

It was hesitantly pointed out to the King that the Palais Royal was not only unfit for use as a theater, but was, in fact, hazardous to enter, since the decayed ceiling beams might momentarily drop on the visitors' heads. But this, too, was solved in an instant. Monsieur Ratabon was ordered to continue demolition of the Petit Bourbon, but simultaneously to start a complete renovation of the Palais Royal, to enable Molière's company to begin performances within the shortest possible time.

Naturally, Monsieur Ratabon no longer had any choice

but to launch an immediate reconstruction of the Palais Royal.

This was the theater where that great lover of the stage Cardinal Richelieu had presented in 1641 an extraordinarily sumptuous production of *Mirame,* of which he was co-author. Despite the technical marvels of the production, the play was one of the worst failures in theater history. By the time of the Ratabon incident, the abandoned hall had fallen into complete decay. The beams had rotted away, the ceilings were full of holes, and the floor was so bad that anyone who stepped on it risked breaking a leg. However, the interview with the King inspired Ratabon with great energy, and while he was renovating the Palais Royal, Molière's company played in the châteaux of the highest French aristocracy. *The Imaginary Cuckold* was shown successfully at the residences of the Maréchal de la Meilleraye, the Duc de Roquelaure, the Duc de Mercoeur, and the Comte de Vaillac.

But Molière had also had occasion during this period to play before still more exalted audiences. Cardinal Jules Mazarin, the King's mentor and Prime Minister of France, had, despite the illness which kept him bound to his chair, expressed the wish to see this new theater which had created such a stir. And on October 26, 1660, the company performed *The Precious Ladies* and *The Bungler* in his château. The Cardinal was pleased. But the performance was enjoyed most of all by a certain young man who concealed himself modestly behind the Cardinal's chair and whom the assembled nobles pretended not to see, although every eye was stealthily drawn to him again and again.

Loret reported somewhat cryptically in his *Gazette et la Muse historique,* "Both plays were greatly enjoyed, and not

[125]

only by Jules, but also by other exalted personages"—the last two words being printed in capitals. Loret went on to say that His Eminence the Cardinal had instructed that two thousand écu be issued to Molière and his company by way of encouragement.

The capitals in Loret's report are not difficult to understand: hiding behind the Cardinal's chair was none other than the King himself, who had for some reason chosen to appear at this performance incognito.

Molière did not delay to take advantage of his success at Court. He obtained permission to transfer from the Petit Bourbon to the Palais Royal not only the furnishings of the actors' dressing rooms, but also two complete tiers of loges. The director wished to transfer to the Palais Royal the stage sets and machinery of the Bourbon as well, but in this he did not succeed. The famous Italian stage machinist Vigarani, who had arrived in Paris to succeed the equally famous Torelli, said that he needed the machines for producing the Royal ballets at the Tuileries. There was a tug of war, and Vigarani won. The machines remained in his hands, upon which the great machinist performed his first miracle, though of a very different order from those expected of him at court. He burnt down all the machines he had won, together with the stage sets, astounding everyone but Charles La Grange. Molière's devoted secretary and treasurer said angrily to his director:

"You know, master, this Vigarani is a regular blackguard! He burnt all the sets and machines to make everyone forget Torelli's work!"

"I can see he is fully a man of the theater, this Vigarani," answered Molière.

And indeed, Vigarani was a man of the theater in the full sense of the word: he could not endure any competitors, which, however, did not prevent him from being a first-rate machinist.

During his enforced guest performances at the châteaux of the aristocracy, Molière had undergone yet another ordeal. Taking advantage of the fact that Molière was temporarily without a theater, the Hôtel de Bourgogne and the Marais did everything they could to tempt his actors away from him. They promised his players mountains of gold, and prophesied that Molière's theater was finished and beyond revival even at the Palais Royal.

Molière was strongly affected by all this. He grew pale, began to cough and lose weight, became suspicious of his actors and looked at them with anxious, pleading eyes. His eyes plainly wondered: would they, or would they not desert him? His condition was noticed, and one day his players came to him, headed by Charles La Grange, and assured him that, in view of his fairness and kindness, as well as his extraordinary talents, he had nothing to worry about—they would not leave to seek their fortunes elsewhere no matter how tempting the offers they received.

Monsieur de Molière wished to make one of those admirably eloquent replies for which he was justly famous, but in his agitation he could find no words and contented himself with shaking hands with everyone. After which he withdrew to meditate in solitude.

Chapter 16
The Sad Tale of the Jealous Prince

Don't force your talent!

—La Fontaine

During this period of his life, Molière made the serious mistake of listening to the evil spoken of him. The insults which he should have ignored cut him to the quick. From the very moment his comedies and the short farces with which he accompanied the longer plays appeared on the stage, the literary gentlemen of Paris began to say in chorus that Molière was an empty buffoon, incapable of treating serious themes. And there were dozens of people who repeated it. True enough, this view was rejected by certain individuals, among them the famous and highly talented fabulist La Fontaine, who subsequently became one of Molière's best friends. After Molière's first performances, La Fontaine exclaimed:

"This is a man after my own taste!"

Molière, said La Fontaine, was magnificently faithful to truth and nature. However, instead of paying attention to

[128]

La Fontaine, Molière listened to critics of quite a different order. And he resolved that he would prove to the world his ability to treat eternal themes, like jealousy, which he had used to comic effect in *The Imaginary Cuckold,* in a serious vein as well. To this end, he would bring forward a hero belonging to the highest social strata. And so, he composed a heroic comedy under the title of *Don Garcia of Navarre, or the Jealous Prince.*

The superintendent had meantime completed the Palais Royal. Everything was put in order, and a vast pale blue cloth was stretched under the ceiling, serving a dual purpose: to charm the viewer's eye with the illusion of an artificial sky, and to keep rain from dripping on him, since the ceiling continued to leak despite Monsieur Ratabon's repairs.

On January 20, 1661, Molière's troupe established itself at the Palais Royal. It was followed by the Italian company, which had returned to Paris. Once again the days of the week were divided between the two companies, but this time the Italians paid Molière, to compensate him for the expenditures incurred in refurbishing the theater. These expenditures, it must be said, had been incurred because the funds allotted by the treasury had proved insufficient.

The Palais Royal was flooded with light, and the dark forebodings that the theater would not regain its place were dissipated at once. The public responded enthusiastically to Molière's plays, and it became clear once and for all that they put into the shade the plays of all the other playwrights.

Everything seemed to be going well until the appearance of *The Jealous Prince* on the stage on February 4. Enormous sums had been spent for the lavish production, and the director of the company himself, who had evidently forgotten how he had been pelted with apples, came forward in the role of the magnificent prince.

The public prepared itself eagerly to view Monsieur de Molière's new work, and listened with benevolent attention to Elvire's first monologue, delivered by Marquise-Thérèse du Parc. Then the Prince appeared and began his flowery monologues about glorious dangers, Donna Elvire's shining eyes, and other elevated subjects. The monologues were so long that the audience found ample time for an unhurried examination of the azure sky and gilded loges of the Palais Royal. Molière played on, but his heart was uneasy: the box office had brought in six hundred livres, and the theater was far from filled. The bored audience waited for something interesting to develop, but we must regretfully admit that nothing did, and in the end the lights dimmed over the jealous prince to the accompaniment of a few scattered hand-claps.

Experienced playwrights know that the success or failure of a play cannot be determined by questioning friends or reading reviews. There is a simpler way—checking the box office. And this Molière proceeded to do. He learned that the second performance netted five hundred livres, the third, one hundred and sixty-eight, and the fourth, four hundred and twenty-six. Then Molière added the triumphant *Imaginary Cuckold* to *Don Garcia* and collected seven hundred and twenty livres. But next time even *The Imaginary Cuckold* did not help, and the evening produced only four hundred livres. And, finally, came February 17, and the ill-omened figure seven, which played such a fatal part in Molière's life.

On Thursday, February 17, at the seventh performance

of *Don Garcia,* the box office produced seventy livres. The director's last doubts were dissipated: both the play and he himself in the role of Don Garcia had suffered a total and irreversible fiasco. He played the prince so badly that even before the seventh performance he had begun to think of turning over the role to someone else.

The fiasco was accompanied, as a playwright's failure always is, by the wild gloating of enemies, the lugubrious sympathy of friends, which is much worse than the joy of enemies, laughter behind one's back, obituaries for the writer's talent, and mocking homemade couplets.

Molière drank the full cup of all this in reward for his flight into high society and the composition of a cold, interminably long play.

"These bourgeois don't know a thing about art!" growled the director without a trace of justice as he removed the sumptuous costume of the prince and returned to his proper self, that of Jean-Baptiste Poquelin. He ended with a fit of coughing and threats to withdraw *Don Garcia* from the Palais Royal repertory and present it only at Court performances. Who but the princes themselves, he evidently thought, could understand the feelings of a prince?

He fulfilled his threat a year later, presenting *Don Garcia* at Court, where it failed as thoroughly as it had at the Palais Royal. Then, no longer saying anything, the director decided to transfer some of the verses, the better ones, from *Don Garcia* to his other plays. There was no sense in letting the material go to waste altogether. And ever after that he could not abide the slightest mention of *The Jealous Prince.*

[131]

Chapter 17

After the Demise of
the Jealous Prince

An important event took place in the beginning of the year
1661. Cardinal Mazarin died on March 9, and on the very
next day the twenty-three-year-old King Louis XIV stunned
his ministers.

"I have summoned you, gentlemen," said the young King,
looking unblinkingly at his ministers, "to tell you that the
time has come for me to take the reins of state into my own
hands. You shall assist me with your counsel, but only
when I request it. Henceforth, I forbid you to sign any
document without my command, be it even the most in-
significant passport. You shall report to me on your work
daily in person."

The ministers, and all of France, immediately realized
how serious a man sat on the throne. This was also realized
by Molière, who knew at once where he would have to
seek protection in the event of difficulty. And such difficulties could easily occur—as had been demonstrated by the incident of *The Precious Ladies*.

In the spring of that year Molière completed his new

comedy, *The School for Husbands.* The play dealt with the triumphant passion of two young people which overcame all obstacles set in its way by rude and despotic old age.

The comedy, ending in a scene with lanterns and a notary signing the marriage contract, was first played in June, with Molière in the part of Sganarelle, and La Grange in the part of the young lover, Valère. It was a brilliant success, *Don Garcia* was forgiven and forgotten by the public, and *The School for Husbands* ran fifty-eight times that season, more than any other play.

One evening the director of the company was sitting in his room, with the text of *The School,* prepared for publication, on the table before him. Molière was writing a dedication to his patron, the King's brother:

"Monseigneur! I offer France two utterly incomparable things. There is nothing greater and fairer than the name I inscribe at the head of this volume, and nothing humbler than its contents."

Molière put down his quill, trimmed the wicks of the candles, coughed, and thought to himself: "But why am I saying this about my comedy?" He sighed, stroked his eyebrow with the feather top of the quill, wrinkled his face, and continued:

"I may be told, perhaps, that this is like placing a crown adorned with pearls and diamonds upon a clay statue or building magnificent porticoes and triumphal arches at the entrance to a wretched hovel. . . ."

"Add more flattery?" the playwright muttered. "No, it could not go much further." He went on:

"I have ventured, Monseigneur, to dedicate this trifle to Your Highness."

And he signed: "The most devoted, most obedient, most loyal servant of Your Royal Highness, Jean-Baptiste Poquelin-Molière."

"That will be fine," the most devoted servant said with satisfaction, without noticing, in the heat of composition, the extraordinary ambiguity of his words about the clay statue and the jeweled crown. For indeed, why would the comedy necessarily be symbolized by the clay statue, and the name of Orléans by the crown?

But be that as it may, the dedication was dispatched to the Duke and met a favorable reception. After which the company set about preparing for important events in the fall.

The history of mankind has known many embezzlers. But one of the most brilliant of them was unquestionably Nicolas Fouquet, the Vicomte de Vaux and Marquis de Belle-Isle, who occupied at the time described by us the post of the Superintendent of Finance in France. Few people had succeeded in looting a state treasury on so grand a scale. If we are to believe evil tongues, Fouquet had in the end lost all conception of where state moneys ended and his own began. The things that went on in the Ministry of Finance under Fouquet defy description. Allocations for payment were made from funds already expended, reports were filled with falsified figures, bribery was rampant.

Fouquet was not a niggardly hoarder; he was a generous, elegant embezzler. He had a succession of mistresses, he gave banquets, he surrounded himself with the best artists, thinkers, and writers, including La Fontaine and Molière. The architect Lovis Le Vau built such a magnificent château for the talented minister in his Vaux estate that even the

French, accustomed as they were to lavishness in that lavish age, were astounded. The walls in the Vaux château were decorated with paintings by the famous artists Lebrun and Mignard. Gardeners planted such parks and gardens around the château, embellished with such fanciful fountains, that a visitor felt that he must surely be in paradise. But Fouquet did not stop at that, and, as if vaguely sensing the events to come, bought the entire island of Belle-Isle and erected a fortress on it, which he staffed with a military garrison.

By the time that *The School for Husbands* was winning its resounding success, Fouquet was already known as the maker of destinies. And the maker of destinies decided to arrange an entertainment for the King at his Vaux estate. Whenever Fouquet did anything, he did it on the grandest scale. In anticipation of his Royal guests, he had a theater built in a silver fir wood, invited the best theatrical machinists and fireworks technicians, and prepared vast quantities of provisions.

Unfortunately, makers of destinies are able to dispose of all destinies but their own, and Fouquet was unaware that the King, with the sole aid of a certain financial expert, Colbert, was at that very moment checking the records of his Ministry of Finance. This audit was conducted secretly and with utmost speed, for Cardinal Mazarin as he lay dying advised the young King to engage the great specialist Colbert in order to catch Fouquet in his machinations. The King was young, but he was a man of cold intelligence, and he looked on calmly as Colbert, who had studied the Ministry's affairs in detail, showed him both the true and the falsified records.

Meantime, Fouquet, led on by his fate, completed the

preparations for his own ruin by inscribing across his château the Latin device: QUO NON ASCENDAM? (Whither Wilt Thou Not Rise?).

And so, at midday on August 15, King Louis XIV, accompanied by his brother, his brother's wife, the Princess Henrietta, and the Queen of England, arrived at Vaux. Witnesses say that the King's usually impassive face darkened as he raised his eyes and saw Fouquet's device. However, it immediately resumed its normal expression. The festivities proceeded as planned, opening with a breakfast for five hundred persons. This was followed by theatrical performances, ballets, masquerades, and fireworks. But what interests me is not so much the breakfasts and firework displays, but how Molière managed, in the course of fifteen days, to write, rehearse and produce an entire play in verse, *The Bores,* commissioned by Fouquet. Nevertheless, he did, and the play was presented on August 17.

By this time Molière had evidently learned enough about the King of France and his tastes. The King was extremely fond of comedy, but even more fond of ballet. *The Bores* was therefore composed as a combination of comedy and ballet. Properly speaking, *The Bores* was not a play in the full sense of the word, but a series of unconnected satirical skits portraying a variety of characters from high society.

It may be asked: how did Molière venture to present to the King pictures of his courtiers done in an ironic vein? Molière's assessment of the situation was precise and entirely accurate. The King had no special fondness for the higher nobility and did not regard himself as the first among the nobles. In Louis' mind, his power was divinely ordained and he himself stood apart and immeasurably above the rest of mankind. He dwelt somewhere in heaven, in the direct neighborhood of God, and he was extremely sensitive to the slightest attempt on the part of any of the higher aristocrats to rise above his appointed level. In short, Fouquet would have done better to slash his own throat with a razor than inscribe the façade of his château with the motto he had chosen. Louis remembered the Fronde, and held the upper nobility in an iron fist. In his presence, it was entirely safe to ridicule the courtiers.

And so, the curtain fell in the garden of Vaux, and Molière appeared before the Minister's guests. He was flustered, without makeup, and dressed in his ordinary clothes. Bowing in confusion, he began to apologize because, in view of the shortage of time, he had not managed to prepare a suitable entertainment for the great monarch. But before Molière, the best of stage speakers in Paris, completed his apology, the cliff on the stage split open, and a naiad emerged in the midst of a cascading fountain (such was the mastery of the machinist Vigarani)! No one would have said that this enchanting divinity was already forty-three! Madeleine, everyone said, was lovely in the role. She began the prologue:

> To see the greatest monarch in the world,
> O, mortals, I have risen from the grotto . . .

When she uttered the last word of the prologue, the oboes in the orchestra sang up stridently, and the ballet-comedy began.

At the end of the performance, the King beckoned to Molière and, pointing at the master of the hunt, Soyecourt, whispered with a smile:

"Here is an original you have not yet copied. . . ."

Molière clutched his head, laughed, and whispered:

"Your Majesty's powers of observation . . . How could I have missed him?"

Overnight he introduced a new scene into the comedy, depicting the passionate deer hunter Dorante, who could talk of nothing but the horses of the currently fashionable horse dealer Gaveau and the dashing exploits of the well-known hunter Drécar. Everyone present gloatingly recognized in Dorante the luckless master of the hunt.

This incident gave Molière the pretext for writing a letter to the King, filled with numerous compliments. He began by saying that he regarded his own self as one of the impossible "bores." Secondly, he wrote that the success of his comedy was due solely to the King, for as soon as the King approved it, everyone else followed suit. Thirdly, that the scene with the hunter, introduced at His Majesty's command, was unquestionably the best in the play, and that, generally, no scene in any of his plays had given him as much pleasure in the writing as this one.

Meantime, while the playwright was improving his play, another play was opening in the parks of Vaux—not a comedy this time, but a drama.

One day, as the King was strolling down a garden path, his companion picked up a letter someone had dropped on the sand. The King became curious and the letter was shown to him. Alas! It was a tender message from Fouquet to a certain Mademoiselle de La Vallière. It can be vouched that, had Fouquet glanced at that moment into the eyes of the King, he would immediately have abandoned his guests and fled from France, taking with him nothing but a purse of gold and a pair of pistols. The point is that the unassuming little gentlewoman, Louise de La Vallière, was known to be Louis' mistress.

Even as a young man, Louis possessed enormous self-control. Hence Nicolas Fouquet spent that August in unruffled calm. The King went on to Fontainebleau, and in early September proceeded to Nantes, where the Royal Council was held. When the Council was over, and the weary Fouquet came out into the street, someone touched his elbow. The Minister started and looked around. Before him stood a captain of the musketeers.

"You are under arrest," the captain said quietly.

These words marked the end of Fouquet's life. After that came his martyrdom, first at the Vincennes prison, and then in the Bastille. His embezzlements were investigated for three years, and when the Court assembled, it was no longer a magnificent Minister who stood before it, but a trembling, unshaven prisoner. Among the judges he saw his bitterest enemies, appointed to the Court by the King himself. Nine of the judges demanded the death penalty for Nicolas Fouquet. Thirteen others, more humane, sentenced Fouquet to lifelong exile. The King, however, disagreed with the sentence and changed exile to life imprisonment.

Fouquet spent fifteen years in prison. He was never taken out for exercise, never permitted to read or to write, and never allowed a visit from his wife and children. It was only in 1680—whether because something stirred in the King's heart, or because the image of the modest La Vallière had been forgotten, replaced by other women—that the King signed an order for Fouquet's release from prison. This order was never carried out. Fouquet did not live to benefit from the King's mercy and left the prison for regions where, as he undoubtedly hoped, another Judge would mete out justice to him, the dishonest Minister, to his vengeful King, and especially to the unknown person who had dropped the letter on the sand.

I must note yet another circumstance. In the preface to *The Bores,* published after the downfall and arrest of Fouquet, Molière did not hesitate to say that the verses of the prologue belonged to the pen of Monsieur de Pellisson, although the latter was Fouquet's secretary and closest friend.

Paul Pellisson conducted himself with equal courage, composing an entire work, *Speeches,* in defense of Fouquet and thus showing that, whatever their faults, he did not betray his friends. The King read Pellisson's work with close attention and dealt mildly with the author: Pellisson was sent to the Bastille for only five years.

Chapter 18

Who Is She?

GERONIMO: An excellent match! Get married quickly.
—*The Forced Marriage*

On February 20, 1662, a wedding took place at the church of Saint Germain l'Auxerrois, which Monsieur Ratabon had not yet managed to demolish.

Before the altar, next to the stoop-shouldered, coughing director of the Palais Royal troupe, Jean-Baptiste Molière, stood a young woman of about twenty. She was homely, with a big mouth and small eyes, but extremely attractive and coquettish. The young woman was dressed in the very latest fashion, and stood with her head proudly thrown back.

The organ boomed over the couple, but neither the waves of organ music nor the familiar Latin words reached the mind of the groom, which had no room for anything but his passion for his bride. Behind the bridal pair stood the Palais Royal actors and a group of relatives, among whom could be seen the aged, gray-haired Royal Upholsterer Jean-

[141]

Baptiste Poquelin, the mother of the Béjarts, Madame Hervé Béjart, Madeleine, with a strange, stony face, and the young Louis Béjart.

This consuming passion had tormented Molière until he finally attained his object: Mademoiselle Menou, also known as Armande Béjart, was standing next to him at the altar.

The marriage contract states definitely that the bride is Mademoiselle Armande-Grésinde Claire Élisabeth Béjart, daughter of Madame Marie, née Hervé, and her late husband, Sieur de Belleville.

But we, who have come to know well the entire family of the late Béjart-Belleville and his spouse, Marie Hervé-Béjart —their eldest son, Joseph, their daughters, Madeleine and Geneviève, and their youngest son, Louis—would like to make closer acquaintance also of the youngest, Armande, who is now about to become Molière's wife.

Since the marriage contract, drawn up in January of 1662, says that the bride is twenty or approximately so, traces of her birth should be sought in 1642 or 1643. And such traces are, indeed, found. A document dated March 10, 1643, attests to Madame Marie Hervé's renunciation of the legacy left by her late husband, Béjart-Belleville, in view of its great burden of debts. The document names all of Marie Hervé's children, that is, Joseph, Madeleine, Geneviève, and Louis, and also a little girl, as yet unbaptized, and hence newly born.

This, of course, is the very same Armande who is now standing at the altar. Everything tallies. She is approximately twenty years old, and she is the daughter of Marie Hervé. Everything would thus be quite clear, were it not for another circumstance. In the statement of renunciation Marie Hervé's children are persistently and repeatedly described as "minors." One cannot help wondering at the civil official who drew up the document, as well as at the esteemed witnesses who attended the signing, and who included two attorneys, one coach-master, and one tailor. The point is that in 1643 the elder son, Joseph Béjart, was twenty-six, and Madeleine about twenty-five! Neither Joseph nor Madeleine could ever have passed anywhere, or under any code of laws, as minors.

What can this mean? It means that the document of 1643 contains false information and, hence, is quite worthless. And if this is so, then a dense shadow of suspicion falls also upon this mysterious, still unbaptized girl.

Madame Marie Hervé was born in 1590. This would mean that she gave birth to the child in her fifty-third year, after an interruption of thirteen years, since Louis was born in 1630, and there seems to be no mention of any other children after that. Could this be possible? Possible, yes, but not very probable. What is entirely impossible, however, is for none of the Béjarts' close friends or numerous acquaintances to have mentioned on any occasion the rather odd circumstance of the aging mother of a family presenting her dying husband with a new child. No child of Marie Hervé is registered anywhere during that period save in the document of 1643.

And how, indeed, could it be registered? Where was it born? No one knows. It is true that in the winter of 1643 the Béjarts left town for a time. This journey coincides precisely with the girl's birth. But why would Marie Hervé need to leave Paris to give birth to a child under conditions that well deserve to be described as mysterious?

Where was the child baptized? No one knows. Her bap-

[143]

tismal certificate could not be found in Paris. Hence, she was baptized somewhere outside of Paris, possibly somewhere in the provinces. To go on: why was the girl spirited away somewhere immediately after birth? Why was she placed with strangers instead of being raised at home, like all the other children?

What conclusion do all these tangled circumstances suggest? A simple and sad one: Marie Hervé did not give birth to any child in 1643, and she lied in the document, claiming for herself a child that was not hers. What, then, could have prompted her to do so?

Since there is obviously little sense in assuming maternity of an altogether strange child, the suspicion arises that this mysterious girl was born to one of Marie Hervé's unmarried daughters. It was this that caused the unexplained departure, this was why the child was secreted away and not brought up at home! But which of the two daughters was the mother? Was it Geneviève or Madeleine? No indication is to be found anywhere ascribing maternity to Geneviève. On the other hand, everyone was always convinced that Armande was Madeleine's daughter, and no one ever thought of her as the daughter of Marie Hervé. And were it not for the discovery of the marriage contract, where Armande-Grésinde Claire Élisabeth Béjart is named as Marie Hervé's daughter—a discovery which mixed up all the cards —no one would ever have mentioned Marie Hervé as the mother.

The well-known writer Brossette wrote in his memoirs: "I was told by Monsieur Despréaux that Molière had first been in love with the comedienne Béjart, whose daughter he later married."

The anonymous author of the pasquinade entitled *The Famous Comedienne* wrote of Armande Béjart-Molière in 1688: "She was the daughter of the late Béjart, a comedienne who enjoyed vast popularity among the young men of Languedoc at the time of the happy birth of her child."

In short, many persons said in Molière's lifetime and wrote after his death that Armande was Madeleine's daughter. But, in addition to these oral and written reports, there are many subtle, if indirect, proofs that Madeleine was Armande's mother.

When Molière married Armande, he received—as can be seen from the marriage contract—a dowry of ten thousand livres from Marie Hervé. But after she had lied in the document of 1643, we have the right to disbelieve her. Marie Hervé did not and could not have possessed ten thousand livres. This money, as was later established, was given to Armande as a dowry by Madeleine Béjart, the only wealthy member of the family. But why could Madeleine not have been generous with her sister? The point is that her generosity was too unequal. When Geneviève was married, two years after Armande's marriage, she received a dowry of five hundred livres in cash and some three thousand livres' worth of linens and furniture.

When Madeleine was dying, she willed Geneviève and the lame Louis small lifetime pensions, but she left Armande thirty thousand livres.

When Mademoiselle Menou unexpectedly appeared in the south, as out of nowhere, Madeleine surrounded her with such solicitude that none of the company believed the relationship to be merely sisterly. Only a mother could lavish such care on a child. And here we must add that there is

[145]

no doubt whatever that Menou and Armande are one and the same person. If it were not so, we would know of Menou's death; besides, we could not then explain Armande's appearance in Paris.

What conclusion can we draw, then?

The conclusion is this: in 1662 Molière married the daughter of Madeleine Béjart, his first, unwedded, wife—the very same Armande who was falsely described in the certificates as the daughter of Marie Hervé.

But who was Armande's father? The first suspicion falls upon Sieur Esprit-Raymond de Moirmoron, Comte de Modène, whom we know as Madeleine's first lover and the father of her child Françoise. But it immediately becomes clear that this suspicion is unjustified. There is a good deal of evidence showing' that at one time Madeleine had been very anxious to have Comte de Modène legitimize their liaison. This was why she had not only made no attempt to conceal from the world the birth of Modène's daughter, Françoise, but had, on the contrary, acknowledged the fact in the birth certificate. The appearance of a second child would have bound Modène to her still more securely, thus furthering her marriage plans. There was no reason for Madeleine to conceal this child and attribute it to her mother. Her action this time, however, was evidently prompted by altogether different circumstances: Madeleine wanted to conceal the child from Modène.

The point is that Chevalier de Modène, together with Louis de Bourbon, the Comte de Soissons, and the Duc de Guise had plotted in 1641 against Richelieu and had been wounded in the battle of Marfée on July 6, 1641. In September of the same year the Parliament in Paris condemned

Modène to death, in consequence of which he went into hiding, first in Belgium and later within the borders of France, but avoiding Paris. This lasted until 1643, when, amnestied after the deaths of Richelieu and Louis XIII, Modène was able to return to the capital.

It must be noted that the Béjart family, fearful of persecution by the government because of its close connection with Modène, also left Paris. However, the wanderings of the Béjarts took place in other regions than those where Modène concealed himself. Obviously, then, Modène would have come to Paris to find Madeleine, after a two-year separation, with another's baby in her arms, and this would, of course, in no wise further his relationship with her.

Modène was definitely not Armande's father. Her father, therefore, must have been some gentleman who was close to Madeleine in the summer of 1642, when she was in the south of France. Madeleine might have met many men at that time, and she might have been intimate with one of them, but the trouble is that among the others—and we know it with absolute certainty—she met Jean-Baptiste Poquelin, the King's Valet and Royal Upholsterer, who was a member of King Louis' suite. This was at the watering place in Montfrin, where Louis XIII was taking a mineral cure, in the latter half of June, 1642.

Well, then, this meeting in Montfrin and the unquestionable intimacy of Poquelin and Madeleine at that time gave rise to the most appalling rumors which were spread about Molière in later years.

The author of *The Famous Comedienne* wrote: ". . . she [Armande] was considered Molière's daughter, although he later became her husband."

[147]

When Armande was called into court as a witness in someone else's case several years after Molière's death, the attorney of one of the parties tried to disqualify her in an acrimonious speech, asserting publicly that she was the former wife and widow of her own father.

A great deal of importance was attributed to a letter from Chapelle to Molière, which contained such mysterious lines as "you will show these excellent verses only to Mademoiselle Menou, particularly since they portray both you and her. . . ."

Certain circumstances suggest that Armande's marriage took place after such painful and terrible scenes between Molière and Madeleine and between Armande and Madeleine that life became intolerable to those three and Armande was compelled virtually to escape to the house of her future husband.

Official documents show that Geneviève Béjart did not attend either the signing of the marriage contract or the wedding, and many people suspect that this was done in protest against this dreadful marriage.

In short, rumors crept all about Molière, poisoning his existence with the accusation that he had committed the gravest crime of incest and married his own daughter.

What can be said about this tangled affair, with its falsified documents, indirect evidence, speculations, and dubious data? My conclusion is this: I am certain that Armande was Madeleine's daughter, that her birth was secret, in an unknown place, and from an unknown father. There is no convincing proof that the rumors of incest were justified and that Molière married his daughter. But neither is there any evidence to disprove this terrible rumor.

There he is, then, my hero, standing before the altar with a young woman half his age, of whom it is said that she is his own daughter. The organ booms over them gloomily, foretelling sundry miseries for this marriage, and all these prophecies, alas, will be fulfilled!

After the wedding, the director of the Palais Royal left his apartment on the rue Saint Thomas du Louvre and moved with his young wife to the rue de Richelieu, taking along with him his valet, Provençal, who was the bane of his existence, and his maid servant, Louise Lefebvre. And there, on the rue de Richelieu, troubles besieged the family without much delay. It soon became apparent that husband and wife were totally unsuited to one another. The aging and ailing husband still passionately loved his wife, but his wife did not love him. And their life quickly became a veritable hell.

Chapter 19
The Playwright's School

Whatever transpired in the Molière apartment on the rue de Richelieu, life at the Palais Royal continued on its course. New actors joined the troupe that year. The first was François Lenoir, Sieur de la Thorillière, former captain of the cavalry, who was not only a talented actor, but also a man of great business experience, which led Molière to entrust him with certain administrative duties. The second was the brilliant comedian Guillaume Marcoureau, Sieur de la Brécourt. This actor was also a playwright, as well as a notorious duelist and a veteran of numerous scrapes.

The season following Easter of 1662 was quiet, for the public had already seen Molière's first plays and the box office fell off. The only plays that stirred greater interest were *The School for Husbands* and Boyer's *Tonaxare*. And so it went on until December, when Molière introduced his new play, the five-act comedy *The School for Wives*.

Like *The School for Husbands, The School for Wives* was written in defense of women and their right to their own choice in love. It presented the tale of the jealous and despotic Arnolphe, who wished to marry young Agnès. In this play replete with comic situations we find, for the first time in any of Molière's plays, a note of bitterness, expressed in the role of Arnolphe.

When the young Agnès triumphs in the end and leaves him with her lover, Arnolphe, repulsive and ridiculous as he is, suddenly becomes pitiful and human.

"Nothing can match my love for you!" Arnolphe cries passionately, as though suddenly divesting himself of the mask of meanness and possessive jealousy. "Ungrateful girl, how can I prove it to you? Shall I cry bitter tears? Or beat my chest? Or tear my hair? Or would you have me kill myself? Just tell me, tell me what you want, and I am ready, cruel one, to prove my passion to you!"

The public noticed this monologue and many people commented, some with sympathy, others with gloating, that it reflected Monsieur de Molière's personal feelings. If this was so, and, alas, it was so, it shows how badly things were going at the rue de Richelieu.

The School for Wives was performed superbly. In addition to Molière in the role of Arnolphe, high plaudits were won by Brécourt in the role of the servant, Alain.

It must be said that, whatever incidents attended the presentation of Molière's previous plays, they dimmed to insignificance in comparison with the things that transpired after the premiere of *The School for Wives*. The premiere itself was marked by a scandal. A certain Monsieur Plapisson, a faithful habitué of Paris salons, who had a stage seat, was outraged by the play to the depths of his soul. At every witticism or stunt, he turned his apoplectic face to the parterre, shouting furiously:

[151]

"Laugh, parterre! Go on, laugh!"

And he shook his fists at the public. Naturally, the laughter rose to an even higher pitch.

The play elicited instant enthusiasm, and the public thronged to the following performances, producing such record-breaking box office figures as fifteen hundred livres an evening.

And what did the Paris literati and connoisseurs of the theater say about the new play? Their first response is difficult to make out, for the salons buzzed with so much abuse at Molière's expense that it was impossible to distinguish the words. Those who had ranted against Molière before were now joined by dozens of new critics. With deep regret it must be admitted that even so great a man and writer as Corneille gave way to the shabby feeling of embittered envy.

As regards the actors of the Hôtel de Bourgogne, they went about like lost souls after the very first performances of *The School for Wives*. But they, of course, had sound reasons for chagrin. Something unheard-of had happened: with the appearance of this play the box office at the Bourgogne suffered a sharp decline.

And then, many naïve individuals throughout Paris went about telling everyone that it was they whom Molière had had in mind when he created the character of Arnolphe, the hero of his comedy. These men, indeed, deserved to be paid by the Palais Royal for raising its box office figures!

And so, the play had caused quite an uproar, in which it was difficult to distinguish the isolated voices of Molière's friends, who could be counted on the fingers. The only voice that was loud and clear was that of Boileau-Despréaux:

> Let the scolding of the envious
> Flow like a muddy river.
> Your delightful comedy
> Is sure to live forever!

Things went badly. A young writer, Jean Donneau de Visé, was the first to comment in print on *The School for Wives*. De Visé's article clearly shows that its author's soul was torn in two as he composed it. De Visé wished first of all to say that the comedy could not succeed, but this he was unable to say, since it was a magnificent success. Therefore, de Visé said that the comedy's success was merely due to the excellent performances of the actors, which shows that de Visé was not a fool. He went on to state that he was grieved by the multitude of ribaldries in the comedy, remarking, by the way, that the plot was poorly constructed. But since, as I have said, de Visé was not a fool, he was obliged to admit that the play, after all, had some few merits and that some of Molière's characters were so vivid as to seem drawn from life.

It appears, however, that de Visé reserved the most important thing for the end of the article, where he announced that a new play, bearing on Molière's *The School for Wives,* would soon open at the Bourgogne. He announced it so slyly that, although he did not name the author, it was clear that the new play would be a product of the pen of Monsieur de Visé himself.

And how did Molière conduct himself all this while? To begin with, he dedicated *The School for Wives* to the Princess Henrietta of England, the wife of his patron, the King's brother. In this dedication, as his custom was, he spilled a bucketful of flattery on the Princess. But after that

[153]

Molière committed a fatal error. Forgetting that a writer must never enter into any published controversy with regard to his works, and brought to the point of exasperation, he decided to attack his enemies. Since he had command of the stage, he delivered his blow from the stage, presenting in June, 1663, a short play entitled *The Critique of The School for Wives.*

This play, in which Armande Molière received her first major role, that of Élise, ridiculed Molière's critics. Following his undeviating rule of always securing his rear at Court, Molière dedicated this play, in most complimentary terms, to the Queen Mother, Anne of Austria. However, the Queen Mother did little to help Molière in the events that followed.

The public gleefully recognized in Lysidas Monsieur de Visé. Another part of the audience cried that it was not de Visé, but a living portrait of Monsieur Edmé Boursault, another literary gentleman and a bitter enemy and detractor of Molière's.

Lysidas-de Visé saw red when *The Critique* appeared and quickly brought forth his own promised play. It bore the rather long title of *Zélinde, or the True Critique of The School for Wives, and a Critique of the Critique.* It portrayed a certain Élomire (an anagram for Molière), who, in a lace shop where the action takes place, eavesdrops on other people's conversations. Much as the Hôtel de Bourgogne wished to produce the play about Élomire, it nevertheless had to abandon it, for on closer examination, it proved to be total nonsense. De Visé had to content himself with printing his work and disseminating it in Paris, whereupon it transpired that the play *Zélinde* was not so much a piece of dramatic criticism as a most ordinary and dangerous denunciation.

[154]

De Visé asserted that the ten old maxims which Arnolphe seeks to impress upon Agnès in preparation for their marriage are nothing else but a clear parody on the Lord's Ten Commandments. Monsieur de Visé, as you see, replied to Monsieur de Molière in a most serious vein.

"The scoundrel," hissed de Molière, clutching his head. "To begin with, there are not ten maxims! Arnolphe begins the eleventh!"

And his head hummed with the words of Arnolphe's rules:

> When a duly wedded wife
> Comes to share her husband's bed,
> She must get into her head . . .

"But he begins the eleventh!" Molière cried to his actors.

"He begins," Molière was told quietly, "but not a single word is uttered, except the words 'Maxim Eleven,' so that, dear master, the listener remembers precisely that there were ten."

I may add at this point that, fortunately, de Visé was evidently ignorant of the source from which Molière derived those ten rules of connubial conduct! For he derived them from the writings of the Holy Fathers of the Church themselves!

Events, meantime, sped on, and hatred for Molière among the literati grew more violent daily. One of the reasons for this was the circumstance that, following the appearance of *The School for Wives,* the King awarded Molière an annual pension of one thousand livres in recognition of his contribution as a great comic writer. The pension was small enough, for scholars and writers usually received much more; nevertheless, it fanned the flames. The relations between Corneille and Molière were now totally ruined. To be sure, this was caused not so much by the pension as by the overwhelming success of *The School for Wives,* as well as by a certain trifling fact: without any malicious intent, but simply in jest, Molière had introduced a line from Corneille's tragedy *Sertorius* into the finale of the second act, giving it to Arnolphe, which made Corneille's line sound comic.

This trifling jest (Arnolphe, speaking to Agnès, uses Pompey's words: "Enough! I am master! Go and obey!") could not have harmed Corneille in any way, but he was extremely wrought up over such treatment of his tragic verse.

Molière's next lessons were still more painful. It was said in the higher circles of society that Molière had satirized two persons in his *The Critique of The School for Wives:* Jacques de Souvré, knight of Malta, and the Duc de la Feuillade, marshal of France and commander of a guards regiment. The affair with Jacques de Souvré had no unpleasant results, but the de la Feuillade business ended badly. Egged on from every side, Feuillade had finally become convinced that it was indeed he whom Molière lampooned in his *Critique* in the character of a marquis who kept repeating with stupid indignation a single senseless phrase: "Cream tart, cream tart!" Angered in the extreme, he subjected Molière to a severe humiliation. When the two met in a Versailles gallery, de la Feuillade, pretending that he wished to embrace the playwright, seized his head and crushed it to his chest so forcefully that Molière's face was scratched to blood by the jeweled buttons of his caftan.

[156]

It is bitter to think that Molière did not repay the Duke for the insult. Whether it was timidity, or the difference in the social positions of a comedian and a duke, or perhaps fear of angering the King, who was a most determined enemy of dueling (Molière himself always ridiculed duelists in his comedies), Molière did not challenge the Duke to a duel. Had this happened, however, Molière's career would have ended with *The Critique,* for de la Feuillade would unquestionably have killed him.

De Visé's play did not reach the Bourgogne stage, but the other victim of Molière's ridicule in *The Critique,* Edmé Boursault, was more fortunate. His play *The Portrait of a Painter, or the Counter-Critique of The School for Wives,* was produced by the Hôtel de Bourgogne. In *The Portrait,* Boursault presented Molière as a highly dubious character and also mentioned the Ten Commandments. The King, however, was quite indifferent in the matter of the Commandments, and Paris began to say that he was following with much interest the war that had broken out between Molière and the whole phalanx of his enemies, and that, indeed, he had himself advised Molière to attack his enemies again from the stage. Alas, the King had given him bad advice!

Monsieur de Molière wrote a play, *The Versailles Impromptu*, which he presented on October 14, 1663. The action was in the form of a rehearsal of a play to be performed before the King, so that the Palais Royal actors played themselves. But the "rehearsal" merely provided Molière with an opportunity to come forward with attacks upon his enemies of the Bourgogne.

The point is that people began to say more and more out-

rageous things about the insulted comedian with the mutilated face. All Paris was, of course, aware by this time of
Molière's unhappy marriage. Evil tongues spread the gossip
that Armande had long been unfaithful to him. Molière's
most painful secret was that he, who had ridiculed the
Sganarelles and the Arnolphes, was himself agonizingly
jealous. It is easy to imagine how he was affected by this
gossip, which exposed him to public disgrace. He decided
that the source of this disgrace was the Bourgogne theater,
and, blinded by rage, he proceeded to ridicule it in *The
Impromptu.*

"Which of you plays kings?" Molière asked, playing
himself. "What? This slender, elegant young man? You
must be joking! A king should be as big and fat as four
men put together! A king must have a paunch, the devil
take it! A king must possess a vast circumference, so he
may properly fill the throne!"

He should not have done this, he should not have mocked
the physical defects of Zacharie Montfleury!

Then followed parodies on the declamation of the actress
Beauchâteau and the actors Hauteroche and de Villiers.
Nor did the marquises escape Molière's barbs:

"Just as in the old comedies," he said, "we always saw a
buffoon servant who made the public roar with laughter, so
in all our plays now there must be a ridiculous marquis to
entertain the audience!"

Then he went on to Edmé Boursault, describing him as a
petty scrivener . . . Yes, the King had unquestionably given
Molière poor advice! But our hero evidently felt like a
solitary wolf who senses the hot breath of pursuing dogs
behind him at the hunt.

[158]

And everyone descended upon the wolf in chorus: de Villiers, together with de Visé, composed a play, *The Marquises' Vengeance,* and the younger Montfleury, Antoine-Jacob, offended to the depths of his soul by the attack upon his father, wrote the play *The Hôtel de Condé Impromptu.*

The Vengeance no longer made any bones about treating Molière as a vulgarian who stole his ideas from others, and called him an ape and a cuckold. And in his *The Impromptu,* Antoine-Jacob Montfleury repaid in full for Molière's treatment of his father: he savagely ridiculed Molière in the role of Caesar, and not without good cause, for, as we know, Molière was execrable in this role.

After that the Théâtre du Marais joined the fray and also derided Molière in a play.

In conclusion, a certain Philippe de La Croix composed a work entitled *The Comic War, A Defense of The School for Wives*, in which he justly remarked that while Apollo slumbered in heaven, writers and actors fought like a pack of dogs. However, commented de la Croix, putting the words in the mouth of Apollo, the play which had caused the war—namely, *The School for Wives*—was a good play.

The wretched year of 1663 ended with the vicious act of the enraged Zacharie Montfleury, who sent the King a formal denunciation of Molière, accusing him of having married his own daughter.

This denunciation stunned Molière completely. No one knows what proof Molière presented to the King to clear himself of the charge of incest, but there is no doubt that such proof had been required. Perhaps he showed the documents naming Armande Béjart the daughter of Marie

Hervé-Béjart. Whatever may have passed between them, the King was entirely satisfied with Molière's argument and the affair went no further. Whereupon the great war between Molière and his enemies began to subside.

What my hero brought out of this war was illness. He developed a suspicious cough and suffered fatigue and a strange state of mind, and it was only later that this state of mind was recognized by medicine as a condition with a very sobering name—hypochondria. And he had also carried to immortality on his own shoulders two minor writers, de Visé and Edmé Boursault. They had dreamed of fame, and won it thanks to Molière. Were it not for his battle with them, we scarcely ever would recall the names of de Visé, Boursault, and many others.

Chapter 20

The Egyptian Godfather

The worm of misery gnawing at his heart, his face scarred by de la Feuillade's buttons, Molière entered the year 1664 in the full glory of his fame, which, having spread throughout France, rose over the Alps and overflowed into other lands as well.

Whatever the domestic troubles of the Molières, Armande gave birth to a boy on January 19, 1664. In the period between the infant's birth and christening, Molière prepared and produced a new comedy, *The Forced Marriage*. Properly speaking, it was a one-act play, but, knowing the King's great love of the ballet, Molière introduced into it numerous dance interludes, expanding it to three acts.

Molière's namesake, the most talented Court composer, Florentine-born Jean Baptiste Lully, composed the music for *The Forced Marriage,* and the Royal Ballet Master Pierre Beauchamps produced the dances. The play required elaborate settings and a great deal of money was spent on it, but that money was not spent in vain.

Molière introduced the ballet to please the King. To

please himself he introduced two comic philosophers. The old Clermont alumnus had not forgotten the lessons of the late Gassendi, and portrayed on the stage two learned dunces: Pancrace, of the Aristotelian school, and Marphurius, a follower of the skeptical school of Pyrrho.

The first sent the audience into paroxysms of laughter by spouting endless streams of wild absurdities. The second, on the contrary, was sparing of words and so skeptical that he urged Sganarelle to doubt even things that a man endowed with eyes could not possibly question. Thus, on arriving anywhere, Sganarelle was not to say "I've come," but "It seems to me that I've come," which, naturally, threw the sensible Sganarelle into just bewilderment.

Two magnificent scenes with this pair of pedants irritated the Paris Faculty of Philosophy, and it is a wonder that no scandal ensued, since, as I have said earlier, it was extremely unsafe to mock philosophers of the Aristotelian school.

The writing of *The Forced Marriage* may have been prompted by a recent adventure of the Count Philibert de Gramont which had created a furore in Paris. This count enjoyed such phenomenal success among the ladies that the tales of his exploits finally wearied the King, and he commanded de Gramont to go to England for a time. But on arrival in England, the Count instantly conquered the heart of a Court lady, a certain Miss Hamilton.

London society, which did not know de Gramont very well, began to speak of a forthcoming marriage. However, when his temporary exile ended, de Gramont prepared to return to his native France and, in parting with the lady, did not say a single word to suggest any marriage plans.

The Count had already reached Dover and was on the

point of embarking when two brothers of Miss Hamilton made an appearance at the pier. A single glance at them was sufficient to convince the Count that the brothers had serious intentions. The ends of their swords peeped out from under their cloaks, as usual, but in addition to the swords they were armed with pistols. The brothers bowed to de Gramont with a civility that seemed to him excessive.

"Count," said the eldest, "have you forgotten anything in London?"

The Count felt on his face the breath of the wind which moved so pleasantly toward his native land, looked at the ship's masts and sails, then at the pistols, and thought to himself: "It's obvious that, even if I succeeded in shooting the elder one, I'd have to fight the younger one. There would be a most tiresome fuss in the port, and, worst of all, it would upset His Majesty in the extreme. Besides, Miss Hamilton is an enchanting young lady . . ."

And the Count politely replied to the Hamiltons:

"Yes, sirs, I forgot to marry your sister. But I am returning to London immediately to repair this oversight."

A short time later the Count was married.

It is also possible that Molière drew the material for his comedy not from Philibert de Gramont's adventures, but from a work by the famous satirist Rabelais, who described the exploits of a certain Panurge.

The sumptuous comedy-ballet was presented on January 29 at the King's chambers in the Louvre with great brilliance. In one of the ballet interludes in the second act, the role of the First Egyptian was danced by the King of France, together with the Marquis de Villeroi. So great was the King's love of the ballet! Also participating in the play, in addition to the King, were his brother, who played one of the admirers of Sganarelle's wife, and a large number of courtiers, of whom three portrayed gypsies and four devils. And everyone without exception said that the best performance in the entire spectacle was that of the First Egyptian. We shall remain silent, but to ourselves we think that best in the show were Sganarelle in Molière's performance, and Pancrace and Marphurius, performed by Brécourt and Du Croisy.

From the Louvre the play was transferred to the company's own stage at the Palais Royal in its one-act form, without the expensive ballet, but it did not enjoy any notable success.

The King gave himself another opportunity to enjoy his favorite art, dancing on February 13 in another ballet, produced for him by the members of the Bourgogne, consumed with jealousy of Molière. The famed Desoeillets and Floridor took part in the prologue to the ballet. And Molière was able to return to his current repertory and his family affairs.

These affairs were full of gloomy secrets and sorrows. and only the gleam of the lamps in the same church of Saint-Germain-l'Auxerrois on February 28 dissipated somewhat the darkness of life for Molière, who was in a state of deep melancholia. That day was marked by the baptism of Molière's firstborn. Everything was arranged with extraordinary pomp and elegance. Beside the baptismal font stood a soldier of the Guards with a long halberd, and the priest's face bore an expression of solemnity and exaltation. The point was that the King of France had consented to be the infant's godfather. The King was represented by the Duc de Crécy, and the most illustrious godmother, Henrietta, the Duchesse d'Orléans, by the wife of Marshal du Plessis. The child was, understandably, named Louis.

The christening produced a great impression in Paris, and the abuse at Molière's address was visibly dampened. Everyone began to see the King's shadow behind the shoulders of the director of the troupe, and many of those who like to be on the side of the winner took to telling with relish that Montfleury with his denunciation had not even obtained a hearing in the palace and had, indeed, been virtually thrown out.

In the meantime, Molière had made a move which struck many people as very strange. He left his apartment on the rue de Richelieu and moved back with his wife to the house on the corner of the Place Royal and rue Saint Thomas du Louvre, where Madeleine Béjart and Madame de Brie were living. After moving, Molière continued, despite his deep depression, to work feverishly on a long play. He did this work secretly and very few people knew about it. Among these were the famous critic and poet Boileau-Despréaux, who had become one of Molière's best friends despite the considerable differences in their ages (he was fourteen years younger than Molière), and one of the cleverest and most interesting women in France, Ninon de Lenclos, who was nicknamed the French Aspasia, and in whose salon Molière had, without undue publicity, read excerpts from his new comedy.

The King, who was now following with benevolent interest the work of his godson's father who had charmed him with his ballets, was most humbly informed by Molière that he was writing a long comedy about a sanctimonious hypocrite.

[165]

During that period, in the spring of 1664, the reconstructions of the Versailles palace were completed, and grandiose entertainments were initiated to celebrate the event.

A cortege moved down an endless avenue between two walls of clipped greenery. It was led by King Louis astride his horse. Orchestras followed, with trumpets blasting so loudly that it seemed they must be heard in Paris, many *lieues* away. Between the orchestras moved chariots, in one of which stood Charles Varlet La Grange, dressed as Apollo. The other chariots bore actors in costumes representing the signs of the zodiac. After them walked costumed knights, blackamoors, and nymphs. In a chariot among these rose the goat-footed god of the woods, Pan, represented by Monsieur de Molière.

What was the meaning of all this? The heralds' trumpets announced the beginning of *The Pleasures of the Enchanted Isle*, a series of grand festivities organized by the Duc de Saint Aignan at the King's command.

The Royal gardeners had carved entire theaters in the Versailles sea of greenery and adorned them with garlands and ornaments of flowers. The pyrotechnists prepared firework displays of unprecedented brilliance and explosive force, and Vigarani devised the machinery for the theatrical performances.

When the festivities began, varicolored lights illuminated the gardens of Versailles every evening, stars rained down with a deafening clatter, and from a distance it seemed that the Versailles woods were on fire.

Molière worked as in a fever for this celebration, and in a very short time composed a play, *The Princess of Elis,* borrowing the plot from some Spanish playwright. In this elegant and empty entertainment, the role of the Greek princess was played by Armande Molière, and the entire Court discovered what enormous talent Molière's wife possessed, and what an excellent schooling she had received from him. Her acting elicited universal admiration, and the Court gallants swarmed around the witty, sharp-tongued woman in lemon-yellow silks embroidered with gold and silver.

The Princess was enormously enjoyed by the King, but to its author it brought new tribulations. The young, handsome, and wealthy cavaliers were a new danger, which poisoned the holidays for him altogether. Gossip about his wife sprang up immediately, on the very first day, and did not delay in reaching Molière's ears, either in the form of biting sympathy or in the form of ugly hints. But he no longer even snapped back, and merely bared his yellowed teeth like a wolf. He had evidently become accustomed to a good deal since the previous year's war with the Bourgogne, and no longer rebelled at being so totally exposed to the eyes of strangers. Besides, a new misfortune struck his house: the King's godson, Louis, died immediately after the premiere of *The Princess of Elis*.

The festivities meantime proceeded, Lully's melodies were played in the flower-decorated theaters, fires dripped from the sky, and the sixth, fateful day of *Les Plaisirs* was approaching. On that day, May 12, Molière, having first warned the King that the play was not yet finished, showed the Court and the King three acts of this most mysterious play about the pious hypocrite, called *Tartuffe*.

I'll make it short. This play portrayed the most complete and consummate swindler, liar, scoundrel, informer, and spy—a hypocrite, lecher, and seducer of other men's wives. And this personage, clearly a danger to surrounding society, was none other than a priest. All his speeches were interlarded with honeyed, pious maxims, and in addition to that, he accompanied his reprehensible actions at every step with quotations from the Holy Writ.

I shall not add any more. This play was performed before the King, the Queen Mother, a most devout woman, and numberless courtiers, many of whom were zealous members of the recently notorious Society of the Holy Sacrament, which had been so relentlessly active in guarding the religious and moral purity of the country that even the government had at one time attempted to ban it.

As the comedy about Tartuffe opened, it was met with warm and benevolent attention. But this immediately gave way to utmost perplexity. And by the end of the third act the audience no longer knew what to think, and the idea flashed in some of the viewers' heads that Monsieur de Molière was, perhaps, not entirely of sound mind.

Of course, there may be all kinds of priests. Take, for example, Abbé Roquette, later the bishop of Autun, whom Molière had known in those unforgettable Languedoc years when Roquette distinguished himself in the eyes of his flock by his remarkably vile conduct. Or the former lawyer Charpy, who had become a preacher while at the same time seducing the wife of the Court Apothecary. Or the well-known Franciscan monk of Bordeaux, Father Itier, who had won wide notoriety during the Fronde by his unprecedented treacheries. Or many others. Nevertheless, to portray on stage the things that Molière portrayed . . . No, you must agree, this seemed impossible to one and all!

[168]

The long-suffering marquises had already grown accustomed to the fact that the King had thrown them, as it were, to Molière's mercy. The Sganarelles, the shopkeepers, had also received their due. But in *Tartuffe* Molière invaded an area where no invasion was permitted.

Indignation was immediate, and it expressed itself in stony silence. An unprecedented thing had happened. With a stroke of his pen, the comedian of the Palais Royal disrupted the Versailles festivities: the Queen Mother demonstratively left Versailles.

Events took a serious turn. The King suddenly found before him the fiery mantle of none other than the Archbishop of Paris, Cardinal Hardouin de Beaumont de Péréfixe, who insistently and emphatically pleaded with the King to place an immediate ban on performances of *Tartuffe*. The Society of the Holy Sacrament repeated again and again that Molière was too dangerous. It was the first, and perhaps the only time in the King's life when he felt at a loss after a theatrical performance.

And the moment came when the two men were alone. For a time they regarded one another in silence. Louis, who had been known from his earliest childhood to express himself succinctly and clearly, felt that no words would somehow come from his tongue. Pushing out his lower lip, the King looked out of the corner of his eye at the paling comedian, and his mind was filled with a single idea: "But this Monsieur de Molière is quite an interesting phenomenon!"

At this point the comedian permitted himself to say the following words:

[169]

"And so, Your Majesty, I wish most humbly to beg your permission to present *Tartuffe*."

The King was stunned.

"But, Monsieur de Molière," said the King, looking into his eyes with great curiosity. "Everybody maintains unanimously that your play ridicules religion and piety . . ."

"May I venture to say to Your Majesty," the father of the King's godson replied in heartfelt tones, "piety may be true, or it may be false . . ."

"True," said the godfather, his eyes never leaving Molière's, "but, again, if you pardon my frankness, everyone says that in your play it is impossible to tell whether you mock true piety or false. You must kindly pardon me, I am not an expert in these questions," the ever-polite King added.

They were silent a while. Then the King said:

"I will have to ask you, therefore, not to present this play."

The festivities having come to so unfortunate an end, the King departed on May 16 for Fontainebleau. Molière followed him, and he in turn was followed by the steadily unfolding matter of *Tartuffe*.

The Fontainebleau performance of *The Princess of Elis* was attended by, among others, the legate and kinsman of the Pope, Cardinal Chigi, who had come to France for talks. *The Princess* pleased the Cardinal, and Molière managed to obtain an invitation to read *Tartuffe* before him. To everyone's astonishment, the Papal legate graciously commented after hearing the comedy that he found nothing unacceptable in it, and nothing offensive to religion. Molière, his spirits lifted by the Cardinal's comments, dreamed of the possibility of gaining protection for the play from the Holy throne. But this did not follow. The

King had not yet settled properly at Fontainebleau when he was handed a work by Pierre Roullé, the curé of the church of Saint Barthélemy, which had been printed in Paris with utmost speed. This work was addressed "To the Most Illustrious of the World's Monarchs, Louis XIV" and was concerned wholly with *Tartuffe*.

The estimable curé was a man of temperament and expressed himself with entire clarity. In his opinion, Molière was not a man but a demon, clothed in flesh and attired in human garb. And since Molière, as Pierre Roullé asserted, was sure to be consigned to the flames of hell in any case, the said Molière should, without awaiting the hellish flames, be burnt in the presence of all the people, together with *Tartuffe*.

When Molière read Father Pierre's missive, he immediately petitioned the King in desperate terms, begging his protection.

Louis XIV detested being told by anyone what to do. In consequence, Roullé's project for an auto-da-fé met with no success whatever. Indeed, the response to both Roullé and his preposterous proposal was most negative.

At this point there appeared another defender of *Tartuffe* in addition to the Roman Cardinal. It was Prince Condé, rude and unpleasant in his manner, but endowed with a lively and curious mind. At the time of *Tartuffe*'s appearance, the Italians presented their farce *Scaramouche the Hermit*, in which a monk was shown in an extremely unfavorable light. The King, who was still at a loss to understand the *Tartuffe* affair, said to Condé after attending *Scaramouche*:

[171]

"I don't see why they have all pounced like that upon *Tartuffe*. Scaramouche says much more caustic things."

"The reason for this, Your Majesty," answered Condé, "is that in *Scaramouche* the author laughs at heaven and religion, about which these gentlemen don't give a damn. But in *Tartuffe* Molière laughs at them. This is why they are so enraged, Sire!"

But even Condé's defense did not help Molière. And what did the author of the luckless play do? Did he burn it? Or hide it? No. As soon as he recovered from the Versailles scandal, the unrepentant playwright sat down to write the fourth and fifth acts of *Tartuffe*.

Molière's patron, the Duc d'Orléans, naturally made Molière play *Tartuffe* for him, and the first three acts were presented in his château at Villers-Cotterets. When the play was completed, it was played in full before Condé at Le Raincy.

Yes, the play was banned, but it was impossible to stop its distribution, and it began to spread throughout France in handwritten copies. Moreover, rumors about the play reached other European countries, and the Swedish Queen Christina, newly converted to Catholicism and visiting Rome at the time, officially asked France for a copy: the Queen wished to have it produced abroad. The French authorities found themselves in an embarrassing position; nevertheless, they managed under some pretexts to refuse the Queen's request.

When Molière, ill, coughing, and already beginning to be irritated at the sight of people, returned to his Palais Royal affairs from Fontainebleau, he found that the box office at the theater was declining. True, *The Princess of*

Elis was successful enough, but it was too expensive. *The Theban Brothers* by the excellent playwright Jean Racine, who was just then coming into fashion, brought in very little. The loss of *Tartuffe* was a misfortune for the director in every respect.

After another serious blow—the death of the fat du Parc—and his replacement by a new comedian, Hubert, who specialized in old women's roles, Molière began to think of something to take the place of *Tartuffe*.

Chapter 21
May Lightning Strike Molière

Molière plunged himself into the study of Spanish legends. Quarreling with his wife, grumbling and coughing, he sat in his study over old folios and scribbled. The image of the handsome seducer Don Juan Tenorio materialized itself before him during his nocturnal vigils and began to intrigue him. He reread the play by the monk Gabriel Tellez, known under his pen name of Tirso de Molina, and the Italian plays about Don Juan. The theme had spread from country to country and attracted everyone, including the French. Just recently, both in Lyons and in Paris, the French had presented plays about Don Juan and the Stone Guest, transformed by the first translator from the Spanish, who misread the word "guest" to mean "feast," into the Stone Feast.

Molière was carried away by the image and began to write his own *Don Juan*, composing a very good play with a strange, fantastic ending: his Don Juan was swallowed up by the flames of hell.

The play was given its premiere on February 15, 1665. Don Juan was played by La Grange, his servant Sganarelle by Molière, Pierrot by the new comedian Hubert, Don Louis by the lame Béjart, Dimanche by du Croisy, La Ramée by Monsieur de Brie. The two peasant girls seduced by Don Juan, Charlotte and Mathurine, were played by Madame de Brie and Armande, who was pregnant again and in her fourth month.

Already at the premiere, *Don Juan, or the Stone Feast* brought in one thousand eight hundred livres. After that the box office improved steadily and reached two thousand four hundred livres.

The Parisians were all agog over *Don Juan*. It might have been expected that the author who had suffered such a heavy blow in connection with *Tartuffe* would immediately repent and offer the public a work that did not challenge established standards and was therefore entirely acceptable. This, however, was not so. Indeed, the scandal created by *Don Juan* was as great if not greater than the scandal over *Tartuffe*, especially since *Don Juan* spoke from the stage, while *Tartuffe*, after all, was known only to a limited circle.

Molière's hero was a total and unqualified atheist, and this atheist was the wittiest, most courageous and irresistibly attractive man despite his vices. Don Juan's arguments invariably struck as sharply as a sword. And the foil against which Molière set this dazzling freethinker was his base and cowardly lackey, Sganarelle.

The guardians of piety were stunned, but their dismay quickly gave way to rage. The first articles about *Don Juan* began to appear. A certain Barbier d'Aucourt, writing under the pseudonym of Rochemont, demanded exemplary punishment for Monsieur de Molière, recalling by the way the punishment meted out by the Emperor Augustus to the fool who had mocked Jupiter. He also mentioned Theodosius, who threw authors like Molière to wild beasts.

Rochemont was followed by another writer, who remarked that it would be a fine thing if the author were struck down by lightning, together with his hero. After that our old acquaintance, the devout Prince Conti, made an appearance, this time his last. In a special treatise on comedy and actors, he declared that *Don Juan* was an entirely undisguised school of atheism, and the Prince's arguments, we must admit, were quite witty.

"It's inexcusable, after all," he wrote, "to make Don Juan pronounce irreverent speeches, while defense of religion and the divine principle is left to his dunce of a lackey. How could the fool prevail against his brilliant opponent?"

Generally speaking, the wish to see the director of the Palais Royal struck down by lightning from heaven was voiced more and more frequently. The strongest impression in the entire play was produced by the admittedly strange scene between Don Juan and a beggar, in which the former inquires as to the latter's occupation and receives the reply that he spends all day praying for the prosperity of those who give him alms. Don Juan remarks that a man who thus prays all day cannot be badly off, but the beggar repeats that he is in dire need. Then Don Juan comments that he is obviously ill rewarded for his pains and offers him a louis d'or if he will blaspheme. The poor man refuses, and Don Juan gives him the louis d'or, as he puts it, "for love of man."

This scene turned against Molière even those who were fairly well disposed toward him, and the final bolt of lightning with which the author strikes down his hero satisfied

[176]

no one at all. In short, *Don Juan* had but a short life on the stage and was banned after its fifteenth performance.

It may be added, too, that thanks to *Don Juan* Molière provoked yet another corporation of learned men in Paris— the doctors, who were mercilessly mocked in the comedy.

Molière thus entered the dull summer season with a host of new enemies. The wretched, dismal summer dragged on interminably. At home he was drawn into quarrels with Armande, pregnant and grown irritable, and swore furiously and fruitlessly over the declining box office. But fighting this decline after the loss of *Tartuffe* and *Don Juan* was extremely difficult.

When things became unbearable, Molière took refuge in wine and a small company of former classmates, with the addition of La Fontaine, Boileau, and the rising star, Jean Racine, which gathered from time to time either at the Mouton Blanc tavern or at the Croix de Lorraine. Presiding over these reunions was usually the noisy Chapelle, whose happiest pastime was drinking with a company of friends. Were such a company, especially with Molière at the head, to appear in any restaurant in France today, the drinks would surely be on the house!

The theater, meantime, continued its activities. In June the troupe presented a command performance in Versailles of *The Coquette*, by the woman playwright Mademoiselle des Jardins. It was performed in an open-air theater in the garden, and the actors were amazed at the extraordinary number of orange trees decorating the theater.

On August 4 Armande gave birth to a daughter. The infant's godfather was our old acquaintance Esprit-Raymond de Modène, and the godmother was Madeleine. The liaison between the old lovers was long over, and Modène and Madeleine were now bound by a quiet and sad friendship. In honor of the former lovers, their names were combined and the girl was baptized Esprit-Madeleine.

Several days after the birth of Molière's daughter came an event which raised the spirits of the company. On the memorable Friday of August 14, 1665, when the troupe was in Saint-Germain-en-Laye, the King conveyed his most august command to Sieur de Molière: from then on the company was to be under the King's personal patronage and was to be known as the King's Players of the Palais Royal. In connection with this, it would receive an annual allowance of six thousand livres.

The actors rejoiced greatly, and it was necessary to provide a fitting reply to the King's favor. Indeed, Molière would have replied at once, were it not for the fact that he was seriously ill. His entire organism had broken down. He developed debilitating pains in his stomach, evidently of nervous origin, which almost never left him. His cough grew progressively more violent, and once he spat blood. Several doctors were summoned for a consultation. As soon as he felt better, however, Molière performed a dramatic feat such as, we may be sure, no other playwright in the world could duplicate. What he did is beyond understanding: in the course of five days, Molière wrote, rehearsed, and presented a three-act comedy with a prologue. This comedy, performed in Versailles, was called *Love, the Doctor* and was thoroughly enjoyed by the King. After that it was transferred to the Palais Royal, where it began to bring in substantial sums. It also provoked the scandal that had become habitual for Molière's plays.

[178]

This time the entire French medical profession was seriously outraged, for the play portrayed four doctors, all of them pure-blooded charlatans.

What had brought Molière to this quarrel with the doctors? We know that he was constantly, hopelessly, chronically ill, sinking deeper and deeper into the hypochondria that was sapping all his strength. He sought help and ran from doctor to doctor, but found no relief. And he was, perhaps, right in his attacks on the doctors, for Molière's age was one of the sorriest in the history of that great art, medicine. In most cases, Molière's doctors failed in their cures, and their feats of ineptitude were countless. As we have said earlier, they killed Gassendi with their bloodlettings. A short time before, just the previous year, one of the doctors sent a good friend of Molière's, Le Vaillere, to the other world by giving him three doses of an emetic, which was totally counterindicated in his illness. Some time earlier, when Cardinal Mazarin lay dying, four doctors summoned for a consultation became the laughing stock of the Parisians by offering four different diagnoses! In short, in Molière's time medicine was in the dark ages.

As regards the purely external characteristics which distinguished doctors at that time, we may safely say that these men, riding through Paris streets on mules, wearing long, gloomy mantles and beards, and speaking a mysterious jargon, simply begged to be set on the stage in a comedy. And in his *Love, the Doctor* Molière brought four of them upon the stage. Their names were invented for Molière during a light-hearted supper by Boileau, who derived them from ancient Greek. The first doctor was called Des Fonandrès, which means "murderer of people"; the second, Bahys, "one

[179]

who barks"; the third, Macroton, "slow of speech"; and, finally, the fourth, Tomès, or "bloodletter."

What followed was a major scandal, for the audience easily recognized in the four quacks four of the Court physicians, Sieur des Fougerais, Jean Esprit, Guénaut, and Vallot, the latter being not merely a Court doctor, but the King's chief physician. About four years after the presentation of *Love, the Doctor*, this Vallot caused the death of Henrietta, the wife of the King's brother, not by bloodletting, but by prescribing for her a dose of opium extract which proved lethal.

The consultation of the four charlatans on the stage provoked endless outbursts of laughter in the theater, and it is small wonder that hatred of Molière among the physicians reached unprecedented proportions.

As for the box office receipts, they rose sharply. True enough, this was aided in equal measure by certain plays of other writers, among them Molière's erstwhile enemy, Donneau de Visé, who had finally succeeded in writing a good play, *The Coquettish Mother*. Molière made peace with him, accepted the play for production, and it enjoyed substantial success.

But the principal hope was vested in Jean Racine's play, *Alexander and Porus*. It was rehearsed and given its premiere at the Palais Royal on December 4, 1665.

At this point, however, Molière's young friend Jean Racine did something that was a grave blow to Molière. That same December the Palais Royal troupe learned to its dismay that the Bourgogne had begun rehearsals of *Alexander,* and that this was being done with Racine's knowledge. La Grange, who played Alexander the Great, realized that he would have to compete with the great Floridor, and the director of the Palais Royal simply clutched his head in consternation, for it was entirely clear that the income from *Alexander* would drop if there was a parallel production at the Bourgogne.

When Racine was asked to explain why he had given a play already in performance to a competing theater, he replied that he was not pleased with the performance of *Alexander* at the Palais Royal and believed that the play would be more successful at the Hôtel de Bourgogne.

At this point the friendship between the two playwrights was severed as with a knife, and Molière conceived a violent hatred for Racine.

Chapter 22

A Bilious Lover

And seek a corner in a distant land . . .
—*The Misanthrope*

After Racine's betrayal Molière became ill again, and was visited more and more frequently by his physician, Mauvilain, who evidently had a fairly good knowledge of his craft. But even Mauvilain found it difficult to diagnose precisely what ailed the director of the Palais Royal. It would probably be closest to the truth to say that all of him was sick. And it is unquestionable that, in addition to his physical suffering, he was racked by a disease of the spirit, which expressed itself in persistent attacks of depression. He felt as though a dismal gray pall had fallen over Paris. The sick man wrinkled his face, twitched, and took to sitting in his room, ruffled like an ailing bird. At moments he was seized with irritation and even fits of rage. At such moments he could not control himself, became insufferable in his treatment of those around him, and once, infuriated over some trifle, he even struck his servant.

Molière was a difficult patient. He asked for medicines, and Mauvilain generously prescribed a variety of drugs and medical procedures. But the patient was erratic in following prescriptions. He was extremely anxious, tried to understand what was taking place within him, constantly felt his pulse, and depressed himself with gloomy thoughts.

In January of 1666 Racine dealt Molière the final blow. The widow du Parc announced that she was leaving to join the Hôtel de Bourgogne. When he heard this, Molière replied with rage that he saw nothing surprising in it, that Marquise-Thérèse was lured away by her lover Racine.

Whether Mauvilain's medicines had helped, or the organism itself had mastered the disease, by the end of February Molière returned to his regular work at the theater. During the spring months he had written a new play, *The Misanthrope*. It was a play about an honest man who protested against human falseness and was, naturally, solitary as a result. Molière's physician might well have made a thorough study of this work, for it unquestionably reflected his patient's state of mind. But then, Doctor Mauvilain had probably read the play.

Although discerning people recognized *The Misanthrope* as one of Molière's best plays, it had little popular success. The premiere met with a rather cool reception. An acquaintance of Racine who had attended the opening told him gloatingly that *The Misanthrope* was a fiasco, meaning, no doubt, to please him with this information. Significantly, the man who was hated by Molière replied:

"So, you saw it? Well, I didn't. Nevertheless, I don't believe you. Molière could not write a bad play. Go and see it again."

The first performances of *The Misanthrope* produced another incident that caused Molière much anxiety. But then, as we know, it would be difficult to imagine a Molière play opening peacefully. As usual, the Parisians began to look for portraits of prominent persons in the play, and the rumor spread that its hero was none other than the Dauphin's tutor, the Duc de Montausier. This rumor soon reached the Duke, who did not have the slightest conception of Molière's play, but immediately decided that if Molière had chosen to portray him, he surely must have drawn him in caricature. Enraged, he declared that he would thrash Molière to death with his cane at their very first meeting. The Duke's threats were conveyed to the playwright by obliging friends, and threw the man, whose emotional equilibrium was already badly shaken, into a veritable panic.

Molière did everything to avoid meeting Montausier, but the encounter was inevitable. When the King attended *The Misanthrope,* Montausier was also there. Molière decided to remain backstage until they left, but when the performance was over, he was told that the Duke wished to see him. The playwright was so overcome with terror that the amazed messengers had to assure him that Montausier had no intention of harming him. Pale, with trembling hands, Molière presented himself before the Duke. His fear, however, instantly gave way to astonishment. Montausier embraced him with the warmest thanks, declaring that he was flattered to have been the model for the portrait of so noble a man as Alceste. The Duke showered Molière with compliments and ever after treated him with utmost friendliness. The most interesting thing in all this was that, in creating his Alceste, Molière had never thought of Montausier at all.

However, despite the play's excellence and its success with the Court circles, its box office returns remained small, and the actors took to addressing their director in melting tones and begging him to give them something new, especially since *Attila,* which the aged Pierre Corneille had given the Palais Royal, held little promise for the future.

Chapter 23
The Magic Clavecin

The actors' pleas produced results, and on August 6, 1666, the theater presented Molière's new farce, *The Doctor in Spite of Himself*. This delightful farce pleased the Parisians enormously and produced excellent returns, adding up to almost seventeen thousand livres for the season. But Molière himself merely shrugged his shoulders. The farce, he said, was a trifling bit of nonsense. What was needed at the moment was not a farce, but something new for the gala festivities planned for December at Saint-Germain-en-Laye. But here we must take note of an important event which had taken place earlier that year, considerably before these festivities and before the presentation of *The Doctor in Spite of Himself*.

There was in France at that time a children's theater, known as the Dauphin's Comedians. It was directed by Madame Raisin, wife of the organist Raisin. For a time the troupe played in the provinces, then it appeared in Paris. Madame Raisin's husband was evidently an excellent inventor. He devised a clavecin which could play a number

of pieces at his behest without the touch of human hands—
a magic clavecin, in a manner of speaking. Naturally, the
audience was stunned, and the King, who had heard of the
magic instrument, commanded its demonstration at Court.
This demonstration ended in disaster. The Queen fainted
at the first sounds of the clavecin, which played by itself.
The King, however, who was not easily impressed by dubious miracles, ordered the instrument to be opened, and in
the sight of the gasping courtiers a cowering, wretched, and
extraordinarily dirty urchin was pulled out of the clavecin.
The boy, doubled up inside the instrument, had been playing
it from within.

This boy, called Michel Baron, was the son of the late
comedian of the Hôtel de Bourgogne and a member of
Madame Raisin's troupe. The youngsters had given several
performances at the Palais Royal, which revealed that the
orphan boy possessed not only extraordinary beauty, but also
a talent for acting perhaps unequaled by any seen before.

Molière declared to everyone that Baron was the coming
star of the French stage. He obtained the boy's release from
Madame Raisin and took him into his own home for upbringing. Separated from his wife, having nothing in common with her except their apartment and the theater, the
lonely and ill director became extremely attached to the
talented youngster. He pampered him as he would his own
son, tried to correct his unruly and insolent temper, and
taught him the art of the theater, achieving great results in
a very short time.

Baron's presence in Molière's home led to difficulties with
Armande, who conceived a violent dislike for the boy. It is
difficult to know the reasons for her attitude, but it may have

been due in large measure to the fact that Molière had begun to write a special role for Baron, that of Myrtil in the heroic pastoral *Mélicerte,* which he was preparing for the forthcoming Royal festivities.

These festivities, named *The Ballet of the Muses,* opened in Saint-Germain in December. A long ballet, with a libretto by Isaac de Benserade, was presented with brilliant success, especially since the King himself danced in it, and with him, Mademoiselle de La Vallière. But *Mélicerte* was played only once: further performances were broken off as a result of a quarrel between Armande and Baron. On the very eve of the opening, Armande, infuriated either by Baron's impudence or by the smallness of her role as the shepherdess Eroxène, slapped the boy.

Proud as Satan, he rushed off to Molière, declaring that he was quitting the company. Molière almost wept, imploring him to remain, but Baron was obstinate, and the director finally succeeded in persuading him not to disrupt the premiere and play Myrtil just that once. After the performance Baron had the audacity to appear before the King, complaining against Armande and begging permission to withdraw from Molière's troupe.

The King granted his request, and Baron reverted to his original state, resuming his place with Madame Raisin.

Molière was heartbroken. There was no one to take Baron's place in *Mélicerte,* and the play had to be withdrawn. Molière hastily put together a trifling pastoral called *Corydon,* with dancing gypsies, wizards, demons, and so on. *Corydon* became a part of *The Ballet of the Muses,* but it was saved only by the charming music composed for it by Lully.

[188]

In addition, Molière produced a third piece for the festivities, the one-act comedy-ballet *The Sicilian, or Love, the Painter,* which was performed on January 5, 1667.

After the Saint-Germain festivities Molière took to his bed, this time in serious condition. He developed hemorrhages from his lungs. His friends became extremely anxious, and the doctor ordered him to leave Paris. It was good advice. Molière was taken to the country and placed, correctly, on a milk diet. By June he was back on his feet and able to return to the theater and play during the current season.

Chapter 24
He Revives and Dies Again

How strange that our writers of comedy seem to be unable to get along without the government. Not a single play will reach its denouement without it.
—Nikolai Gogol, *In the Theater Lobby*

The year 1667 was important and entirely unlike the preceding dull year. This year the two men whose lives I am following, the King of France and the director of the Palais Royal troupe, had conceived two ideas.

The King's idea was that his wife, Maria Theresa, daughter of the Spanish King Philip IV, who had died two years earlier, had a hereditary right to the Spanish possessions in the Netherlands. And he set himself to developing this idea in full detail.

The idea of the King's comedian was, perhaps, less momentous, but it drew him as irresistibly as the plan to annex more lands to France drew the King. When, thanks to proper treatment, the suspicious pink spots disappeared from Molière's cheeks and his eyes lost their ominously feverish glitter, he took from his bookcase the manuscript of *Tartuffe* and began to revise it. To begin with, he changed Tartuffe's name to Panulphe. Then he divested him of his clerical garb and turned him into a worldly official. Then he eliminated many of the quotes from the Holy Writ, softened the most caustic passages, and thoroughly reworked the finale.

This finale is quite remarkable. When the swindler Tartuffe, or Panulphe, was already on the verge of triumph, when he had ruined honest men and there seemed to be no escape from his clutches, rescue appeared, and it came from the King himself. A virtuous police officer, who springs up from out of nowhere, not only arrests the hero at the last and most crucial moment, but also delivers a most instructive monologue, from which it may be seen that, as long as the King exists, honorable men have nothing to fear and no swindler can escape the monarch's eagle eye. Glory to the police officer, and glory to the King! Without them, I simply cannot imagine how Molière would have finished his *Tartuffe*. Just as I don't know how, one hundred and seventy years later, another ailing satirist* in my distant homeland could have resolved his rather well-known play *The Inspector General* had not a gendarme with a horse-tail on his head galloped in from St. Petersburg just in the nick of time.

When he completed his revisions and reread them with satisfaction, the author began to circle cunningly around the King. And the latter, having in his turn risen to great heights, had begun to circle smoothly in the upper air, his eyes undeviatingly on the Netherlands, spreading below. While Spanish jurists were arguing subtly and in great detail that Maria Theresa, and hence King Louis XIV, had

---

* Nikolai Gogol.—Tr.

no grounds for claiming Spanish holdings, the King, deciding that the affair was being unduly prolonged, brought it out of the juridical plane. He had everything ready. His ministers made sure of agreements with Portugal, England, and other nations, and the air was suddenly filled with that ominous silence which usually precedes an outbreak of great noise. Then Paris grew animated. The richly clad cavaliers suddenly became serious, began to shun diversions, and donned their battle cloaks.

The director of the Palais Royal troupe decided that the moment was propitious. He presented himself to the King with an enchanting smile, showed him the manuscript, told him about his revisions. The King glanced benevolently at his comedian, thinking of something else, and probably muttered something vague to the effect that, actually, he had nothing against the play. . . . Molière's eyes flashed and he instantly vanished from the King's reception hall.

The cavalier de Molière was immediately succeeded by Marshal Turenne, who had been summoned to the King, and before Spain and the Netherlands had time to realize what had happened, the French cavalry burst in upon the Netherlands. The war was on.

Far from the thunder of cannons, Monsieur de Molière and his players, all of them in a state of utmost agitation, rehearsed *Tartuffe* under a new title, *The Impostor*. On August 5, the day of the unforgettable premiere, the public surged into the Palais Royal. The box office returns were nineteen hundred livres, and the play's success was enormous. On the very next day, however, a bailiff of the Parliament of Paris appeared at the Palais Royal and handed

[192]

Monsieur de Molière an official order from Guillaume de Lamoignon, first President of the Parliament, to halt performances of *The Impostor* at once.

Molière rushed to the Duchesse d'Orléans, who sent one of her attendants to the President. The latter replied that, unfortunately, he could do nothing, since there was no permission from the King for the production. Then Molière, with his loyal friend Boileau, who was on good terms with de Lamoignon, paid the President a visit. They met a most courteous reception. The President not only did not torment the author with reproaches or call the play dangerous, but, on the contrary, he gave full due to Molière's talent, uttering numerous compliments. Lamoignon was irreproachably cordial, but in the end he categorically refused to grant his permission to perform *The Impostor* until the King decided the matter.

Molière had never fought so stubbornly for any of his plays as he did for *Tartuffe*. He called his faithful comrade, pupil, and friend La Grange, and with him Sieur La Thorillière, and begged them to find a stagecoach and hurry to the King's headquarters in Flanders.

La Grange and La Thorillière took with them a thousand livres and a long petition from Molière, which was concluded with an appeal to the King to protect him from the frenzy of those Tartuffes whose existence made it impossible to think of composing comedies, even the most innocent. In the same petition Molière assured the King that his only intention in writing the play had been to amuse his monarch after his glorious campaign—to bring a smile to the lips of him whose name made all of Europe tremble. . . .

[193]

Molière embraced La Grange and La Thorillière, and on August 8 the coach bearing them to Flanders disappeared in a cloud of dust.

Tartuffe and *The Impostor* were on all tongues in Paris, and on the eleventh a new misfortune struck. All Paris was reading a message from the Archbishop. It was worded most solemnly, beginning with the following lines:

"It has been reported to us that on Friday, the fifth day of this month, one of the city's theaters presented, under the new title of *The Impostor,* a most pernicious comedy which is all the more dangerous to religion in that, under the pretext of condemning hypocrisy and false piety, it gives encouragement to condemnation of those who manifest true piety as well . . ."

The Parisians gasped, reading the message. Molière's enemies gloated. Those who had not been at the theater on August 5 lamented it. And the Archbishop went on sternly in his message to say that, knowing the danger of insults to piety, particularly at a moment when the great King was risking his life for the sake of his country, a moment that called for fervent prayers for the safety of his sacred person and for victory, he, the Archbishop, forbade not only the performance of this play, but also its reading, either in public or in private gatherings of any kind, under threat of excommunication. The Archbishop further commanded the deans of the churches of Saint Mary Magdalen and Saint Séverin to see that this ban was complied with.

"Issued in Paris, with our stamp affixed, on the eleventh day of August, of the year 1667."

The weight of this message was too great, as even the most naïve people could see, and the Parisians understood that *The Impostor* was a lost cause. Yet Molière made still another attempt to save his cherished work. One of his friends, or perhaps a group of them, issued a letter in defense of *The Impostor,* but the letter was of no avail.

Paris became intolerable to Molière. He discontinued performances at the Palais Royal until the return of La Grange and Thorillière, and withdrew to the village of Auteuil, in the vicinity of Paris, where for four hundred livres a year he rented an apartment from Sieur de Beaufort. De Beaufort placed at Molière's disposal a kitchen, a dining room, a bedroom, two rooms in the attic, and the right to stroll in the park. In addition, Molière took a room for another twenty écu in the event that one of his friends should come to visit him in Auteuil. He agreed with Armande that he would take Esprit-Madeleine with him and place her in a private boarding school in Auteuil. They also agreed that their cook, La Forêt (to whom, as rumor had it, Molière first read his new comedies to see whether or not they were funny), would come to Auteuil whenever Molière had visitors. For his daily needs, he hired a maid, Martine. To the Auteuil attic he brought with him volumes of Plutarch, Ovid, Horace, Caesar, and Herodotus, as well as a treatise on physics composed by his friend Rohault, with the author's inscription.

And so the author of *Tartuffe* disappeared from Paris.

However, the guest room did not remain vacant very long. It was soon occupied by Molière's true and faithful friend Claude Chapelle, who settled down in it, surrounding himself with bottles of wine. He comforted his erstwhile classmate and strolled with him through Sieur Beaufort's yellowing park. In September, when the leaves turned altogether

[195]

yellow, La Grange and Thorillière appeared in Auteuil even before they had time to wash the dust of the road off their bodies. Embracing the director, the messengers reported that the King was in good health, and the campaign was victorious. As for *Tartuffe,* the King had heard the petition favorably, but postponed the question of its performance until after his return.

The King had won his war, and Monsieur de Molière, who had fought as tenaciously for his *Tartuffe,* was defeated. He had revived his Lazarus, but the latter lived only one evening, the evening of August 5.

Chapter 25

Amphitryon

Molière had no fondness for nature or rural existence. Our comedian was truly a city man, a son of Paris. But his unhappy family life and the unceasing efforts of many years had exhausted him, and the Auteuil exile became a necessity for him. He limited his ties with Paris to visits at the Court and the theater. The days when there were no performances were spent in the Auteuil attic, where he watched the Beaufort park changing with the seasons. Chapelle entrenched himself in Auteuil, and from time to time other friends came: Boileau, and La Fontaine, who were often joined by the Comte de Guilleragues, a diplomat and a great admirer of Molière's works, and Marquis de Jonsac, a good friend of Chapelle's.

The visitors came to divert Molière from his work, chat on literary themes, read aloud other people's bad verse, and compose epigrams, including those on the Archbishop of Paris, Hardouin de Péréfixe. Their gatherings usually ended with suppers in Chapelle's room, which delighted everyone, and especially Jonsac.

For one of his suppers, Chapelle had for some reason prepared twice the usual quantity of wine. Molière, feeling ill, merely looked in on the merry company for a moment, refused to drink, and retired to his own quarters. The others feasted until three o'clock in the morning, at which time it became clear to them that life was vile. The speeches were delivered chiefly by Chapelle. Auteuil had long gone to sleep, and the cocks had crowed many hours ago.

"All is vanity, vanity of vanities," Chapelle intoned ominously, pointing an accusing finger into space.

"We quite agree with you," echoed his drinking companions. "Go on, Chapelle!"

Chapelle spilled a glass of red wine on himself, which distressed him still more, and he continued:

"Yes, my poor friends, all is vanity! Look around you and tell me what you see!"

"We see nothing good," Boileau agreed, looking around him with bitterness.

"Science, literature, art—all is vanity, all is worthless!" cried Chapelle. "And love? What is love, my poor unhappy friends?"

"A deception," said Jonsac.

"True!" responded Chapelle, and went on: "Life is nothing but sorrow, injustice and misfortune, which are all around us." And Chapelle wept.

His distraught friends sought to comfort him, but he concluded with a fervent plea:

"And what remains for us to do, my friends? When life is such a dismal pit, it must be left behind without delay! My friends, let us all go and drown ourselves! Look out of the window, at the river! It beckons us to come!"

[198]

"We shall follow you," his friends cried, and the entire company rose, buckling on their swords and putting on their cloaks for the march to the river.

The noise in the room increased. And then the door swung open and Molière appeared, in a nightcap, wrapped in his cloak, with a candle in his hand. He looked at the tablecloth dyed red with wine, at the guttering candles.

"What is going on here?" he asked.

"Our life is unbearable," Chapelle said, weeping. "Adieu, Molière, forever. We are going to drown ourselves."

"An excellent idea," Molière replied sadly. "But it was unkind of you to forget me. I am, after all, your friend."

"He is right! It was rotten of us!" cried the repentant Jonsac. "Come along, Molière!"

The friends embraced Molière and called:

"Come!"

"Well, if that's what we are going to do, let's do it," said Molière. "But there's one thing that troubles me, my friends. It isn't right for us to drown ourselves at night, after supper. People will say we did it because we were drunk. We shall go to bed now and sleep till morning, and at ten o'clock, washed and dressed properly, with proudly lifted heads, we shall walk to the river, so that everybody will see that we drowned ourselves like true philosophers."

"A brilliant thought!" exclaimed Chapelle, embracing Molière again.

"I agree," said Jonsac, and suddenly fell asleep, putting his head down on the table among the glasses.

It took Molière nearly an hour, with the aid of Martine and two servants, to divest the candidates for drowning of their swords, perukes, and caftans and prepare a place to sleep for each of them. When everything was in order, he returned to his quarters. But sleep would no longer come, and he sat up till sunrise, reading.

On the following day the mass suicide was, for some reason, cancelled.

In Indian literature there is said to be an interesting, though highly improper, tale about a god who assumed the likeness of a certain man and seduced his wife in the husband's absence. When the latter returned, the court ordered the two to compete in lovemaking, so that it might judge which of them was the true husband. And, of course, the god was the winner.

The roving theme of a god assuming a husband's likeness was taken up by the Greek author Euripides and by the Roman Plautus. French writers were also fascinated by it. Rotrou composed a play called *The Doubles,* which was presented in 1636. Borrowing from the above authors, Molière wrote a comedy in excellent verse and with original rhymes. It was called *Amphitryon,* and was given its premiere on January 13, 1668. It went through twenty-nine performances that season and brought the highest box office returns. Next in the number of performances came *The Fashionable Widow* by de Visé, who had taken firm root in the theater, Molière's *The Sicilian,* and old Corneille's *Attila.* In box office returns, however, they were far behind *Amphitryon.*

True to his custom of dedicating his plays to highly placed personages, Molière dedicated *Amphitryon* to His Serene Highness Prince de Condé, remarking wittily that it would, of course, be more fitting to place the name of the great Condé at the head of an army, rather than a book.

In honor of the signing of the peace and the annexation of a part of Flanders by France, a great celebration was arranged in the newly landscaped gardens of Versailles. And the Court Dramatist Molière wrote for this celebration a three-act comedy *George Dandin, or the Baffled Husband.* The hero of the comedy was a bourgeois who ambitiously sought to marry into the aristocracy and doomed himself to a life of misery with a wife who brazenly betrayed him.

When the play was finished and Molière's friends learned its contents, they warned him that there was a certain man in Paris who would unquestionably recognize himself in George Dandin. He would surely create a scandal and take some hostile action. Molière thanked them for the warning and said that he would find a way of reconciling this man with his play. On the same evening the experienced director met the man in question at the theater, approached him, and inquired when he might have some free time, for he, Molière, would like to read his new play at his home. The bourgeois gentleman, tremendously flattered, said that he was free any time, even the following evening, and immediately after the performance he paid a series of visits to acquaintances, inviting them for the reading.

"Would you drop in tomorrow," he would say, from one end of Paris to another. "We'll spend the evening together. And, incidentally," he would add with a serious mien, "Molière asked if he may read his new play at my home."

On the following day Molière could barely squeeze

through the crowd of guests at the man's home. After that reading the host became one of Molière's warmest admirers.

George Dandin was soon followed by *The Miser,* one of Molière's great comedies, so that we may safely say that the air of Auteuil was beneficial for the sick Molière. The year 1668 was a fruitful one.

During the last days of that year, on December 11, Marquise-Thérèse du Parc departed this life, winning great glory at the end by her performance of Racine's *Andromaque* at the Hôtel de Bourgogne. The enchanting dancer, who had become a great tragic actress in maturity, departed. And de Molière forgave the treacherous actress all her betrayals and bade her rest in peace.

Chapter 26
The Great Rebirth

Who can illuminate the tortuous paths of a comedian's life? Who will explain to me why a play that could not be performed in 1664 and 1667 could be performed in 1669?

In the early part of that year, the King summoned Molière and said:

"You have my permission to present *Tartuffe*."

Molière put his hand up to his heart, but mastered himself, bowed respectfully to the King, and went out. He started rehearsals at once. The role of Tartuffe was entrusted to du Croisy. Molière himself played Orgon. Madame Pernelle was played by Hubert, Cléante by La Thorillière, Valère by La Grange, Mariane by Madame de Brie, and Elmire by Armande. The premiere of the reborn play took place on February 5. To say that the play was successful would be an understatement. The premiere of *Tartuffe* was a theatrical event in Paris, and the box office returns reached the unprecedented figure of two thousand eight hundred and sixty livres.

[203]

On the day of the premiere Molière wrote a letter to the King:

"Sire!

"A highly estimable doctor whose patient I have the honor to be promises to extend my life for another thirty years if I can obtain a certain favor from Your Majesty. I told him that I did not ask so much of him and would be satisfied if he would only undertake not to kill me.

"This favor, Sire, is the Canon's post in the Royal Chapel of Vincennes, vacant at present. May I venture to ask this additional favor of Your Majesty on the very day of the great resurrection of *Tartuffe,* restored to the stage by Your Majesty's great bounty? By this bounty, I am reconciled with the pious hypocrites. And by it I shall make peace with the doctors.

"Undoubtedly, these are too many favors all at once for me, but perhaps not too many for Your Majesty.

"With respectful hope I shall await an answer to this petition."

The candidate for the Canonry was the son of Doctor Mauvilain.

The King summoned Molière, and once again, as several years earlier, after the first performance of three acts of *Tartuffe,* they were alone. The King glanced at Molière and thought, "How he has aged!"

"What does the doctor do for you?" he asked.

"Sire," replied Molière. "We chat about this and that. From time to time he prescribes medicines, which I don't take as diligently as he prescribes them, and I always manage to get well, Your Majesty!"

The King laughed and Doctor Mauvilain's son instantly received the Canonry to which he aspired.

Tartuffe was performed thirty-seven times that season. When accounts were taken at the end of the season, it was found that *The Miser* brought in ten and a half thousand livres; *George Dandin*, six thousand; *Amphitryon*, two thousand one hundred and thirty; *The Misanthrope*, two thousand; Pierre Corneille's *Rodogune*, the odd sum of eighty-seven livres; and *Tartuffe*—forty-five thousand.

Chapter 27
Monsieur de Pourceaugnac

The people who lived with my hero began to depart this world one after the other. Molière's aged father, Jean-Baptiste Poquelin, died twenty days after the premiere of *Tartuffe*. How far were the days when the beginning comedian would run to his father and throw him into despair with requests for money. Toward the end of his father's life, the situation had changed, and many a time the famous son helped out the old Poquelin in difficult moments.

And so, the father was gone. And the son continued with his own work. In the autumn of 1669 Louis commanded a series of festivities to be arranged in Chambord. For these festivities Molière composed a ballet-farce, under the title of *Monsieur de Pourceaugnac*.

The hero of the farce was a nobleman from Limoges, de Pourceaugnac, who was ridiculed and made a fool of by the Parisians while he was visiting the city. The Parisians said, and evidently with good reason, that the model for Pourceaugnac was in Paris at the time. According to the story, a certain gentleman from Limoges who was visiting Paris had attended the Palais Royal one evening and, while sitting on the stage, conducted himself disgracefully. Annoyed by something, he picked quarrels with the actors and abused them in the rudest manner. In retaliation, Molière portrayed him in his comedy, making him the laughing stock of Paris. It was said that the provincial guest was so outraged when he saw *Pourceaugnac* that he threatened to bring suit against Molière. For some reason, however, he never carried out his threat.

Others said that the absurd gentleman from Limoges made sport of in the comedy was Molière's revenge upon the city where he had once been whistled down and pelted with apples. This is not likely. Would Molière have troubled to avenge something that had happened twenty years before? Besides, it was not only in Limoges that he had been pelted with apples.

The truth is that Limoges and its people had more than once been the object of ridicule, both by Molière and by other authors. The reason for this was that the people of Limoges were known for many unpleasant, absurd, and rude traits, which naturally struck the sharp and observant eye of the Parisian. This was why the citizens of Limoges had even before Molière been satirized in literature and tagged with coarse and ridiculous nicknames.

From the moment when Molière had first attacked physicians in his comedies, he invariably returned to them, finding in the medical faculty an inexhaustible object of ridicule. In *Pourceaugnac,* too, there are scenes with ludicrous physicians and apothecaries. The comedy also sent its share of darts at lawyers. We can thus see that Molière's one-time studies of the law had not been wasted, for he drew on his knowledge to satirize pettifoggers.

By general consensus, Molière's farce was superficial and rather crude, but funny. The part of Pourceaugnac was played by Molière himself, while Hubert performed the female comedy role of Lucette. The farce was first presented on October 6, 1669, at Chambord for the King, and then transferred to the Palais Royal stage, where it enjoyed excellent success. It brought the highest returns of the season, outstripping even *Tartuffe,* which was followed, considerably behind, by *George Dandin* and *The Miser*. The season when *Pourceaugnac* was presented was also remarkable for the fact that, out of thirteen plays performed at the Palais Royal that season, twelve were by Molière.

Chapter 28

The Egyptian Is Transformed Into Neptune, Neptune Into Apollo, and Apollo Into Louis

In the beginning of 1670 the King ordered another series of royal divertissements, at Saint-Germain-en-Laye.

On January 30, the Royal troupe, headed by Molière, arrived at Saint-Germain to present the five-act comedy-ballet, *The Magnificent Lovers,* based on an idea suggested by the King. The characters in this lavish comedy and its intermezzos comprised princesses, military commanders, pagan priests, nymphs, tritons, acrobats on wooden horses, and even dancing statues.

Molière himself played the jester Clitidas, and the dancers in the ballet numbers included many Court gentlemen. Sitting on cliffs, they represented sea gods and tritons, and many of them, including the Duc d'Armagnac, the Marquis de Villeroi, and the Ginguens, both elder and younger, showed great talent in their parts. To the blasting of trumpets and the clatter of pearly shells, the god Neptune rose from the watery depths, and everyone recognized the King. Later, the King changed costume and appeared in the last intermezzo, illuminated by Bengal lights, as the sun god

Apollo. The god Apollo danced, to the accompaniment of the admiring whispers of the courtiers.

Everything proceeded smoothly, and it seemed that the chorus of praise would not be silenced as the festivities went on into the following days, that it would be followed by exquisite poems and the sighs of ladies as they spoke of how enchanting the King was in his Grecian vestment. But an unforeseen incident put an end to all that and greatly upset Sieur de Molière. On the day following the first performance, the ecstatic comments on the King's dances suddenly began to die down, and then ceased completely. The Court journal did not have a word to say about the King's participation in the divertissement. And several days later, when naïve persons asked how the King felt after his performances, the higher courtiers would answer drily:

"His Majesty did not take part in the entertainment."

The reason for this was speedily discovered. It turned out that, immediately after the first performance, the King came upon a newly written tragedy by Racine, *Britannicus,* which contained the following lines about the Roman emperor Nero:

> He struts in plays before the Romans,
> Squandering his voice in the theater,
> Reciting verses and demanding praise,
> While soldiers compel the audience to applaud.

This was all. But after reading this passage, Louis XIV immediately discontinued his appearances in the theater.

"A plague on that Jean Racine!" the director of the Palais Royal cursed hoarsely, coughing and spitting.

When the Saint-Germain festivities were over, Molière

plunged himself into the cares of the current summer season. In April, the lame Louis Béjart, nicknamed Sharp Louis, retired from the troupe. The lame actor had worked with Molière for twenty-five years. He had begun as a boy, following the oxen with Molière in the heat of the southern roads and playing comic young servants. Toward the end of his career, he won high praise for his incomparable performance in the role of the "lame dog," as Harpagon called his rogue of a servant, La Flèche, in *The Miser*. Sharp Louis was weary, and the company, led by Molière, resolved at a special meeting to pay Louis Béjart an annual pension of one thousand livres as long as the company existed. And so Sharp Louis retired.

To replenish the troupe, Molière invited two provincial actors, a husband and wife. Jean Pitel, also known as Beauval, had begun his career as a candle snuffer, and had later risen to the status of actor. His wife, Jeanne de Beauval, specialized in the roles of queens in tragedy and soubrettes in comedy. Molière had to expend a good deal of energy to train the couple in his system and free them of provincial stage mannerisms.

The year 1670 was scheduled as an uninterrupted series of festivities and celebrations in the King's various residences. For a brief moment this chain of entertainments was interrupted by a sad event: the wife of the Duc d'Orléans, Henrietta, died on the hands of the hapless Doctor Vallot. The Court donned mourning, and the preacher Bossuet delivered a flowing sermon over the coffin, which abounded in noble thoughts and drew tears from the eyes of the assembled Court. The grief, however, was cut short that same day, as etiquette prescribed, and the festivities resumed. Horns were blown in the forests of Chambord, and the Court went forth to the hunt. Molière and Lully, who was steadily gaining fame and influence at Court, were commanded to compose an amusing comedy set to music for the Chambord entertainments; this comedy, they were told, was to portray some Turks.

The point of the matter was that, during the preceding fall, the King received a Turkish mission at Versailles, headed by a certain Suleiman Agha. The reception was conducted in a rather striking manner. First, the Turks were made to wait for a very long time. Second, they were received in a gallery of the new palace which was furnished with supernatural elegance. The King sat on a throne, wearing a suit embroidered with fourteen million livres' worth of diamonds.

However, the experienced diplomat Suleiman Agha astonished the Court far more than it had expected to astonish him. Suleiman's face bore an expression which seemed to say that in Turkey everyone wore clothes covered with fourteen million livres' worth of diamonds. In short, the wily Turks refused to be dazzled.

The King was displeased, and the courtiers, accustomed to noting the least mark of emotion in his face, exerted themselves for a year thereafter ridiculing the Turks in every possible way. Hence, the composer and the playwright were instructed to introduce into the play a comic scene involving Turks. The Chevalier Lorand d'Arvieux, who had traveled in the East, was assigned as a consultant to supply the writer and the composer with information on the manners and customs prevailing in Turkey. The three men secluded themselves in Auteuil and developed the plot of the play. It must be said that Molière worked with a vaguely troubled feeling. He began to realize that the main elements in the play would be its musical and ballet portions, while its dramatic aspect would be relegated to the background. He began to fear Lully's power and influence, knowing how his music affected the King.

And it was so that *The Would-be Gentleman* came into being. The hero of the play was the bourgeois Jourdain, who was obsessed with the sweet dream of becoming an aristocrat and an accepted member of high society. Molière's idea was significant and witty. To Jourdain he juxtaposed the Marquis Dorante, and it was obvious in advance that the aristocrats' animosity toward Molière would be intensified to the extreme, since this Dorante was portrayed as a totally dishonorable adventurer, and his mistress, Dorimène, was a shady character at best.

And what about the prescribed Turks? They were there. The thoroughly duped Jourdain was awarded the nonexistent title of a Mamamouchi. He was led out on the stage with his head shaved. Turks marched out to music, led by a mufti, with burning candles in his headdress. The Turks clowned during the ceremony, now dropping on their knees, now rising and intoning meaningless syllables. Jourdain was made to kneel while a Koran was placed on his back, and so on in the same vein. I must say that, personally, I am not in the least enthusiastic over the Turkish parts of the play. I shall leave it to others, however, to judge whether there is anything witty in such lines as those addressed by the mufti to Jourdain. These lines are a melange of Portuguese, Spanish, and Italian words, all of them used ungrammatically (presumably to make them seem funny).

[213]

If you know
You to say.
If not know,
No say, no say.
I—mufti.
And you who are?
No understand?
No say, no say.

In short, I would thank neither the Chevalier Lorand
d'Arvieux for his counsel, nor the Court for its command,
nor the exhausted and worried Molière for the composition
of an intermezzo that spoils a fine play.

The Would-be Gentleman was first played at Chambord
on October 14, 1670, and dark terror gripped Molière after
the performance: the King did not say a word about the
play. Serving the King at the gala supper after the show
in his capacity as Royal Valet, Molière was numb with panic.
The King's silence immediately produced lush results.
There was not a man who did not damn Molière's play
(not in the King's presence, of course).

"Tell me, for God's sake," exclaimed one of the courtiers,
"what is the meaning of all this rubbish, all those 'Hulabas,
baladas, and chabalas' that the Turks cry out? What is it?"

"Gibberish," others replied. "Your Molière is finished,
he has nothing more to say, it's time the theater was taken
away from him."

Alas, we must admit that those "balabas" are indeed
meaningless and there is nothing gay or funny in them.

The play was performed again on October 16, and again
in the presence of the King. After the performance, the King
summoned Molière.

[214]

"I wanted to tell you about your play, Molière," he began.

"Go on, kill me," everybody read in Molière's eyes.

"I said nothing after the premiere because I had not yet formed my judgment. Your actors play too well. But now I see that you have written an excellent play, and none of your other plays has given me as much pleasure."

As soon as the King dismissed Molière, he was surrounded by courtiers showering him with praise. It was remarked that the most extravagant praise came from the man who had said the day before that Molière was finished as a playwright. Here are his words:

"Molière is inimitable!" he cried. "By God, there is extraordinary comic power in everything he writes! Oh, messieurs, he is better than the classics!"

The comedy was repeated in Chambord, and then in Saint-Germain. At the end of November, it was brought to the Palais Royal, where it enjoyed great success and brought in more than twenty-four thousand livres during the 1670 season, taking first place at the box office. Last place during that season was taken by *The Doctor in Spite of Himself,* which brought in the ridiculous sum of one hundred and ninety livres.

Among the events brought by the year 1670 was the death, in the eightieth year of her life, of the widow Béjart, born Hervé, the mother of Madeleine and the woman who signed her name to such strange documents. She had been one of the few who knew the secret of Armande's birth, and she took it with her to the grave.

There was yet another death, which plucked the great Desoeillets from the ranks of the Hôtel de Bourgogne.

In that same year the famous pasquinade of Molière, *Élomire the Hypochondriac, or the Doctors Avenged,* appeared in print. The author of this work was Le Boulanger de Chalussay. *Élomire* recounted every deil of Molière's life and activities and besmirched everything it touched. The very word "hypochondriac" shows how much the author hated Molière, and the contents attest to his close familiarity with many facts of Molière's life. Molière, of course, read this work, but he never made any answer to it anywhere.

I have deliberately left the good things that happened that year for the end. At Easter, after four years of wanderings in the provinces, the seventeen-year-old Baron, matured and dazzlingly handsome, presented himself to Molière. Molière immediately accepted him into the company, assigned him a full actor's share, and gave him the role of Domitian in Corneille's *Tite and Bérénice.* This play took second place, after *The Would-be Gentleman,* in the number of performances and box office returns.

Chapter 29
Collaboration

Molière was commanded by the King to compose a lavish play with a ballet for the carnival of 1671, which was to take place at the Tuileries. Molière immediately began to write *Psyche*. As he worked, attacks of illness and of hypochondria became more and more frequent, and he realized that he would not be able to complete the play in time. He decided to turn to others for help. His relations with Pierre Corneille had long been restored after the quarrel at the time of *The School for Wives*. Corneille and Molière were now bound by their common antipathy for Racine. Old Corneille's star had begun to decline, while Racine's rose ever higher. Racine was played at the Hôtel de Bourgogne, and Molière began to produce Corneille in his Palais Royal.

Molière invited Corneille to collaborate with him on *Psyche,* and the old man, who needed money, willingly accepted. They divided the work as follows: Molière prepared the outline of the five-act play and ballet and wrote the prologue, the first act, and the first scenes of the second and third acts. The rest was written by Corneille, who spent about fifteen days doing it. The sixty-five-year-old man did an excellent job. But even together the two masters would not have finished the work in time. Therefore, a third one was invited—the capable poet and playwright, Philippe Quinault, who composed all the verse to be sung in the play.

The introduction written for this tragedy-ballet is of considerable interest. It states very cautiously that Monsieur de Molière was less concerned in this work with dramatic persuasiveness than with the elegance and beauty of the production. It is said that the introduction was penned by Molière himself.

Psyche was produced with great brilliance at the Tuileries. The best theatrical machinery and flying apparatus were placed at Molière's disposal. Psyché was played by Armande, L'Amour by Baron. Both demonstrated such magnificent acting that they charmed the audience. But the very first performance of *Psyche* in Court on January 17 dealt Molière a new and agonizing blow. A rumor spread and stubbornly persisted in Paris that little was left of Armande's old antipathy for the once impertinent boy, and that, infatuated with the handsome young man and great actor, she became his mistress. The sick and aging Molière endured this in silence.

On March 15 he began a large-scale renovation of the Palais Royal. All the loges and balconies were refurbished, the ceiling was repaired and painted, the stage was reconstructed so that it could accommodate new, complicated stage machinery.

At this point the Palais Royal troupe pleaded with Molière to bring *Psyche* to the theater. After long vacillation, the decision was made, despite the great difficulties entailed

[218]

in the procurement and installation of new machines and elaborate sets. But in the end these difficulties were overcome, along with another problem: until *Psyche,* musicians and singers had never appeared before the public. They played and sang concealed in the loges, behind lattices or curtains. For additional compensation, Molière succeeded in persuading them to appear openly on the stage. *Psyche* was rehearsed for a month and a half and given its premiere at the theater on July 24. All the expenditures and effort were repaid in full. The strikingly lavish production brought surging crowds to the Palais Royal. The play went through some fifty performances that season, and brought in forty-seven thousand livres.

During the period between the presentation of *Psyche* at the Court and its premiere at the Palais Royal, Molière's company played with middling success his farce *The Swindles of Scapin.* This farce was said to be crude and unworthy of Molière's pen. The basis for this judgment is difficult to understand, for this play gave fine expression to Molière's comic gifts. And Boileau was entirely wrong to reproach his friend for descending and pandering to the crowd's tastes, and to criticize the scene where a man is put into a sack and beaten with sticks as a tasteless cliché. Boileau was mistaken: this is a funny, excellently constructed farce, which is not impaired even by the improbable denouement. The comic actors of the Palais Royal, headed by Molière-Scapin, performed it beautifully (the lovers, Octave and Léandre, were played by Baron and La Grange).

That year Molière had no rest. A new command came from the King. Festivities were scheduled for the year's end in honor of the new marriage of the King's only brother.

Molière hurriedly set himself to work on a comedy entitled *The Seductive Countess,* based on his observations of the provincials. The comedy pleased the Court, especially by its intermezzos and ballets.

Chapter 30

Scenes in the Park

The park in Auteuil. Autumn. Leaves rustle underfoot. Two men stroll down an avenue. The elder one leans on a walking stick. He is stooped, he twitches nervously and coughs. The other man, younger, has the rosy face of a connoisseur of wines. He whistles and hums a meaningless song:

"Myrdonden . . . myrdonden . . ."

They sit down on a bench and converse, at first about trifles. The younger man, forty-six years old, talks of how he had thrown himself upon his servant with his fists the other day because the servant was a scamp.

"But he was sober yesterday," says the older man, coughing.

"Nonsense!" cries the younger man. "I repeat, he is a scoundrel!"

"I agree, I agree," the older man replies in a hoarse voice. "I am merely saying that he is a sober scoundrel."

The autumn sky is transparent over the Auteuil park.

After a while, the conversation becomes more animated, and from the window in the house it can be seen that the older man is speaking with great intensity to the younger, who responds from time to time.

The older man says that he cannot forget her, that he cannot live without her. Then he begins to curse his life and declares that he is a wretched man.

Ah, it's a dreadful thing to be the confidant who must listen to other people's secrets, especially their marital secrets! The younger man fidgets restlessly. . . . Yes, he feels sympathy for his companion. But . . . he could do with a drink now! Finally, he begins to criticize the woman without whom the older man cannot live. He says nothing directly, he merely hints at certain painful problems. . . . He alludes in passing to the *Psyche* affair. God forbid, he wouldn't dare to say anything against Armande and . . . Baron. But, generally speaking . . .

"Let me be frank with you!" he exclaims at last. "But this is stupid, after all! A man of your age cannot return to his wife, who . . . well, you must forgive me, who does not love him."

"She doesn't," the older man repeats in a flat voice.

"She is young, flirtatious, and . . . please forgive me . . . empty-headed."

"Go on," the older man says hoarsely. "You can say anything you wish. I hate her."

The younger one merely shrugs, thinking, "The devil take this mess! Now he loves her, now he hates her!"

"I will not live much longer," says the other, and adds mysteriously, "You know how seriously ill I am!"

"Oh, Lord, why did I come with him to the park?" thinks the younger man, and says:

[222]

"Ah, nonsense! I don't feel so well either. . . ."

"I am fifty, don't forget that!" the older man says threateningly.

"Good God, yesterday you were forty-eight," the younger man brightens up. "Really, how can a man get two years older in a day, just because he's in a bad mood?"

"I want to be with her," the older man repeats monotonously. "I want to be back at the rue Saint Thomas!"

"In the name of all that's sacred, I beg you, go into the house! It's too chilly here. Oh, well, after all, what difference does it make to me? Try to make up with her. Although I know nothing will come of it."

The two return to the house. The older man goes in.

"Go to bed, Molière!" the younger man cries after him. For a while he stands by the door, thinking. A window opens, and the older man's head, without his peruke, in a nightcap, appears.

"Chapelle, where are you?" asks the man in the window.

"Well?" replies the other.

"So what do you think?" the man in the window asks. "Should I return to her?"

"Close the window!" says the younger man, clenching his fists.

The window closes, and the man spits and walks away, around the corner of the house. A moment later he is heard calling his servant:

"Hey, teetotaler! Come here!"

On the following day the sun is still stronger, not at all like an autumn sun. The older man walks down the avenue, but now he does not drag his feet and does not turn the rotting leaves with his cane. Next to him walks a man much younger than himself. He has a sharp, long nose, a square chin, and ironic eyes.

"Molière," says the younger man. "You ought to leave the stage. Believe me, it isn't fitting for the author of *The Misanthrope* to be . . . a misanthrope! Oh, this is important! And I hate to think of the author with a bedaubed face, pushing someone into a sack for the amusement of the pit! It is not fitting for you to be an actor. It is painful to see you acting, believe me."

"My dear Boileau," answers the older man. "I will not leave the stage."

"You should be satisfied with your writing!"

"I get nothing out of it," replies the other. "I've never, in all my life, succeeded in writing anything that brought me even the slightest satisfaction."

"Stop being childish!" cries the younger man. "I want you to know, sir, that when the King asked me whom I consider the greatest playwright of his reign, I said it was you, Molière!"

The older man laughs, then he says:

"Thank you from the bottom of my heart, you are a true friend, Despréaux. I promise you, if the King should ask me who is the greatest poet, I will name you!"

"But I am serious!" the younger man exclaims, and his voice resounds through Sieur Beaufort's deserted and beautiful park.

Chapter 31
Madeleine Departs

In the beginning of the winter of 1671 Molière reconciled himself with his wife, left Auteuil, and returned to Paris. He was at that time completing his work on *The Learned Ladies,* which he had written, not to order, but for himself. He worked on it in spurts, now interrupting it, now resuming.

During the days when he was writing *The Learned Ladies,* Madeleine Béjart lay gravely ill in a little room upstairs, in the same house. She had left the theater after playing her last role, that of Nerine in *Monsieur de Pourceaugnac,* after saying her final words on the stage:

"So you've forgotten this poor child? Our little Madeleine, whom you had left me as a token of your fidelity? Come here, Madeleine, my child! Shame your father for his infamy! No, you will not escape! I will prove to everyone that I am your wife, I will make sure you're hanged!"

Madeleine left not only the theater; she turned away from everything worldly, became extremely religious, spent her time in prayer and repentance for her sins, and spoke only to her priest and her notary. In January of 1672 her condition took a turn for the worse. She lay motionless in her bed, over which hung a large crucifix.

On January 9 she dictated her will, in which she bequeathed all she had saved throughout her lifetime to Armande, and left Geneviève and Louis small pensions. She also provided in advance for everything else, ordering masses to be said for her and arranging for five sous to be distributed daily to beggars, in memory of the Lord's five wounds. Having thus prepared herself for death, she called Armande and Molière to her bedside, and, also in the name of the Lord, bade them live in peace and harmony.

On February 9, 1672, the King summoned the troupe to Saint-Germain. In the middle of February, a messenger arrived in Saint-Germain to tell Molière that Madeleine was very sick. He hastened to Paris, and came there just in time to close the eyes of his first beloved and to bury her. The Archbishop of Paris issued permission to give Madeleine a proper Christian burial, since she had abandoned the actor's calling and had been known as a pious woman. And Madeleine was buried in solemn ceremony, after mass at Saint-Germain-l'Auxerrois, at the cemetery of Saint Paul, next to her brother Joseph and her mother, Marie Hervé.

Madeleine died on February 17, 1672. About a month later *The Learned Ladies* had its premiere at the Palais Royal. The more cultivated Parisians rated this play very highly, setting it on a level with Molière's best works. Others criticized Molière sharply, saying that he belittled women in his work and supposedly argued that their education should not go beyond the kitchen.

[226]

The play ridiculed two actual persons: the doctor of theology Abbé Cotin, the enemy of Boileau and author of *The Satire of Satires*; and our old friend Gilles Ménage. The former was presented under the name of Trissotin, the latter, of Vadius.

While the comedians were playing *The Learned Ladies* at the Palais Royal with middling success, a cloud suddenly loomed over the country. On April 7 it broke, and there was war with the Netherlands. Once more, as five years earlier, the French army thrust eastward, and city after city fell under its onslaught. Far from military storms, our Jean-Baptiste de Molière was preoccupied with personal affairs. Now he was a wealthy man, who had accumulated considerable means in the course of his work on the stage. Madeleine Béjart's legacy enriched him further. He took a large apartment on the rue de Richelieu and furnished it with a lavish hand. The lower floor of the two-story apartment was to be Armande's; his own rooms were upstairs. When everything was ready, and all the furnishings were set in place, Molière discovered that the depression that had hounded him at Auteuil had followed him to Paris. His old anxieties and premonitions took up residence with him in his upstairs rooms.

The year 1672 was not going well. Lully had gained enormous influence at Court and was granted privileges to all the dramatic works which featured his music. This meant that Lully now had author's rights to many of Molière's plays, since he had written the music for them.

Molière felt a chill wind blowing at his back. He could not deceive himself: the King was turning from him. The mediocre composer Lully, devoid of any profound ideas of his own, totally subservient to the King's will, had now won Louis' complete favor.

The summer went by gloomily. The husband and wife were intimate again, Armande was expecting a child, but inwardly their relations were in no way improved, and there could be no doubt now that they never would. On September 15 Armande gave birth to a boy, who was hastily baptized and named Pierre-Jean-Baptiste-Armand. But the child lived less than a month. In the winter Molière locked himself up in his upstairs rooms and began to write a new comedy, *The Imaginary Invalid*. To avoid dependence on Lully, he invited another composer, Marc-Antoine Charpentier, to write the music for it.

In *The Imaginary Invalid* Molière mocked the most irrational fear existing among men—the fear of death and obsessive preoccupation with health. His hatred of doctors was at its most violent at the time, and in the comedy they were depicted as veritable grotesques—ignorant, stupid, avaricious and backward.

The prologue written by Molière for this play suggests that he tried to win back the King's favor.

"After the glorious, wearying and victorious exertions of our most August Monarch, it is fitting for all who wield a pen to devote themselves to celebrating his name or diverting his leisure. This is what we have endeavored here. This prologue is intended as a tribute to the great victor, and the comedy that follows was composed to divert the Monarch after his noble labors."

The characters in the prologue were the mythological divinities Flora, Pan, and fauns. The concluding chorus was:

May the thousand-voiced echo sing:
Louis is the mightiest King!
Happy, happy those who can devote their lives to him!

But something must have happened to prevent the performance of this prologue. The King's military fortunes may have turned at that moment, making it necessary to discard the prologue lest it sound like a mockery, or the King may generally have lost interest in his comedian's work. Whatever the reason, the play was presented at the Palais Royal instead of the Court, and instead of the mythological gods, a shepherdess came out and sang a new prologue, which contained the following words:

Ignorant and foolish doctors,
Boasting vainly of your skills!
How can words of Latin cure
The grievous pain that grips me still?

The premiere of *The Imaginary Invalid* took place on February 10, 1673, with great success. The second and third performances were also met with enthusiasm. The fourth was scheduled for February 17.

Chapter 32

Black Friday

ARGAN: Is it not dangerous to play dead?
TOINETTE: No, no. What danger can there be? Hurry, stretch out here!

—*The Imaginary Invalid*

It was a gray day in February. On the second floor of the house on the rue de Richelieu, a man in a bright green robe over his underwear paced back and forth on the threadbare carpet, coughing and groaning. The man's head was wrapped in a night kerchief, like a peasant woman's. The logs burned gaily in the fireplace, and it was pleasant to look at the fire, turning the eyes away from the February murk.

The man paced the study, halting from time to time to examine the engraving on the wall near the window. The engraving depicted a man with protuberant, stern, and intelligent eyes, with a face reminiscent of a falcon, and in a peruke with large, tight rings of hair falling onto his manly shoulders. Under the portrait was a coat of arms—a shield with three flowers.

The man in the bathrobe was talking to himself under his breath, with an occasional caustic smile at his thoughts. When he stopped before the engraving, he softened a little, held his palm over his eyes, squinted, and admired the portrait.

"A fine print!" the man in the robe said to himself reflectively. "I would say, a very fine print . . . the great Condé," he said with emphasis, and then repeated several times senselessly: "The great Condé . . . the great Condé . . ." And then he mumbled: "Print . . . print . . . I'm glad I obtained it . . ."

He crossed the room and sat for a while in the armchair by the fireplace, his slippers discarded and bare feet stretched to the life-giving fire.

"I'll have to shave," he said reflectively and rubbed his stubbly cheek. "No, I won't," he answered himself. "It is too tiring to shave every day."

His feet warmed, he put on his slippers and walked to the bookcases, stopping near one where manuscripts were piled on the shelves. The edge of one sheet hung over the shelf. The man pulled out the manuscript by its corner, and read the title *Corydon*. With a savage smile he tried to tear it, but his hands defied him; he broke a nail, and with a curse stuffed the manuscript among the logs in the fireplace. A moment later the entire room glowed with bright light, and then *Corydon* fell apart into thick black pieces.

While the man upstairs was busy burning *Corydon,* a conversation took place downstairs between Armande and Baron, who had come to visit Molière.

"He didn't go to church," said Armande. "He says he isn't feeling well."

"Why should he go to church?" asked Baron.

"Today is the seventeenth, the anniversary of Madeleine's death," explained Armande. "I went to mass."

"Oh, yes, of course," Baron said politely. "He coughs?"

Armande kept glancing at the guest. His blond peruke flowed to his shoulders in two bright streams. He wore a new silk caftan, his trousers were trimmed with precious lace, his sword hung on a wide band, and on his chest he wore a furry muff. Baron squinted down at the muff from time to time, very proud of it.

"You are all dressed up today," said Armande, and added: "He coughs, and he scolded the servants all morning. I've noticed, Friday is the worst day. But then, I've seen too many Fridays in eleven years. But you had better go upstairs to him, don't sit here, or the servants will again spread heaven knows what rumors throughout Paris!"

And Armande and Baron went to the inner staircase. But before they had time to ascend, a bell began to ring impatiently upstairs.

"Again, ding, ding, ding," said Armande.

The door upstairs flung open, and the man in the robe came out on the upper landing.

"Hey, who's there?" he asked querulously. "Why does the devil always carry them off . . . Ah, it's you? Good afternoon, Baron."

"Good afternoon, Master," Baron answered, looking up.

"Yes, yes, yes, good afternoon," said the man in the robe. "We must have a talk . . ."

He rested his elbows on the railing, propped his cheeks with his hands, and began to look like a funny monkey in a nightcap. Armande and Baron realized with astonishment

[232]

that he intended to talk with them right there, on the stairs, and remained standing. The man was silent a while, then he began:

"I wanted to say this: if my life . . . if misfortunes and pleasures had followed one another in my life in equal measure, I swear, I would have regarded myself a happy man, my dear sirs!"

Armande looked up at him, frowning tensely. She lost all desire to go upstairs. "Friday, Friday . . ." she thought. "Again this hypochondria!"

"Consider yourselves!" the man went on pathetically. "If there is never a single moment of satisfaction, of joy, then what's the good of it? I see very clearly that it's time for me to bow out of the game! I assure you, my dear ones," he added soulfully, "I assure you, I have no more strength to cope with troubles. You know, I have no rest! Eh?" he asked. "And generally, I suppose I will die soon. What do you say to that, Baron?" And he hung his head over the railing.

There was silence on the stairs. Baron did not like the man's words at all. He frowned, glanced quickly at Armande, and said:

"I think, Master, that you should not play tonight."

"That's right," Armande said. "Don't play tonight, you aren't feeling well."

There was a grumbling upstairs.

"What nonsense! How can a performance be canceled? I do not want the workmen to curse me afterward for depriving them of an evening's pay."

"But you are not feeling well," Armande said in a rasping voice.

"I feel excellent," the man replied stubbornly. "But I want to know something else: Why are all those nuns creeping around in our house?"

"Don't mind them, they are from the Saint Clare convent, they've come to beg alms in Paris. Let them stay until tomorrow, they won't annoy you, they'll be downstairs."

"Saint Clare?" The man in the nightcap seemed to be astonished for some reason. "Saint Clare? So what if it's Saint Clare? If they are from Saint Clare, let them sit in the kitchen! Otherwise it looks as if there were a hundred nuns in the house! . . . And give them five livres." And the man suddenly slipped back to his room and closed the door behind him.

"I told you it's Friday," said Armande. "There's nothing to be done about it."

"I'll go up to him," Baron said hesitantly.

"I don't advise it," answered Armande. "Let's go in to dinner."

That evening on the Palais Royal stage ridiculous doctors in black caps and apothecaries with enemas initiated Argan into the medical profession:

> If the sick man
> Barely breathes?

And the new doctor, Molière, cried gaily:

> Give an enema,
> Then bleed,
> Then purge.

The initiate swore twice to be loyal to the medical faculty.

[234]

When the president demanded that he swear a third time, he said nothing, but moaned and collapsed into a chair. The actors started and hesitated. They had not expected this antic; besides, the moan seemed too natural. But the initiate got up, laughed, and cried out in Latin:

"I swear!"

The audience noticed nothing, but some of the actors saw the initiate's face change color, and perspiration appear on his forehead. The surgeons and apothecaries finished their ballet numbers, and the play was over.

"What was the matter with you, Master?" La Grange, who had played Cléante, asked anxiously.

"Oh, nonsense!" Molière replied. "I simply felt a stitch in my heart, but it went at once."

La Grange went to count the money collected that evening and take care of some other business, and Baron, who had not played in the show, came to Molière when he was dressing.

"You felt ill?" he asked.

"How did the audience respond to the performance?" answered Molière.

"Magnificently. But you don't look well, Master."

"I look fine," said Molière. "But I suddenly feel cold." And his teeth chattered.

Baron glanced probingly at Molière, turned pale, and rushed to the door. He flung it open and called:

"Is anyone there? Order my sedan chair brought up, quickly!"

He removed his muff and told Molière to put his hands into it. Molière, suddenly meek, obeyed silently, and his teeth began to chatter again. A moment later he was

[235]

wrapped, the bearers lifted him into the sedan, and took him home.

The house was still dark, for Armande, who had played Angélique, had just returned from the theater. Baron whispered to her that Molière was ill. People began to hurry about the house with candles, and Molière was led up the wooden stairs to his rooms. Armande was giving orders downstairs, and sent one of the servants for a doctor.

Meantime, Baron and one of the maids undressed Molière and put him to bed. Baron was growing more apprehensive every moment.

"Master, is there anything you want? Would you have some broth?"

Molière bared his teeth and said, with a testy smile:

"Broth? Oh, no! I know what my wife puts into the broth; it's stronger than acid."

"Shall I give you your medicine?"

And Molière replied:

"No, no. I am afraid of medicines you have to take internally. Do something to make me sleep."

Baron turned to the maid and whispered:

"A pillow with hops, hurry!"

A moment later the maid returned with the pillow stuffed with hops, and it was slipped under Molière's head. He began to cough, and blood appeared on his handkerchief. Baron stared at his face, bringing a candle close, and saw that Molière's nose had suddenly grown sharp; there were shadows under his eyes, and small beads of sweat stood on his forehead.

"Wait here," Baron whispered to the maid, rushed down-

[236]

stairs, and collided with Jean Aubry, the son of Léonard Aubry, who had once paved the street for elegant carriages. Jean Aubry was the husband of Geneviève Béjart.

"Monsieur Aubry," whispered Baron, "he's very bad, run for a priest!"

Aubry gasped, pulled his hat over his eyes, and ran out of the house. Armande appeared at the staircase with a candle in her hands.

"Madame Molière," said Baron, "send someone else for the priest, but quickly!"

Armande dropped the candle and disappeared in the darkness, while Baron hissed, "Damn it, why isn't the doctor coming?" and hurried back upstairs.

"What shall I give you, Master?" he asked, and wiped Molière's forehead with his handkerchief.

"Light!" said Molière. "And some Parmesan cheese."

"Cheese!" said Baron to the maid, who shifted from foot to foot for a moment, and then ran out.

"Tell my wife to come up," said Molière.

Baron ran down the stairs, calling:

"Who's there? Bring more light! Madame Molière!"

Candles were lit one after another downstairs by someone's trembling hands. Upstairs, meantime, Molière strained his whole body, shook, and blood gushed from his throat, staining the bedclothes. For a moment he was frightened, but immediately he felt great relief and thought, "That's good . . ." Then he was struck with astonishment: his bedroom had turned into an edge of the woods, and he saw a cavalier in black, wiping the blood from his head. Then the cavalier began to pull on the reins, trying to get out from

[237]

under his horse, which had been wounded in the leg. The horse was thrashing about and crushing the man. Strange voices were heard in the bedroom:

"Chevaliers! To me! Soissons was killed!"

"The battle at Marfée . . ." thought Molière. "And the cavalier under the horse is Sieur de Modène, Madeleine's first lover . . . Blood flows from my throat like a river, a vein must have burst somewhere . . ." He began to choke on the blood and his lower jaw twitched. De Modène vanished, and Molière saw the Rhone, at the moment when the world was ending. The bloody disk of the sun began to sink into the water to the sounds of the lute in the hands of Emperor d'Assouci. "Stupid," thought Molière. "The Rhone, and the lute at the wrong time . . . I'm simply dying . . ." He had time to think with curiosity, "How does death look?" And he saw it immediately. It ran into the room in a monastic headdress and made the sign of the cross over Molière with a sweeping movement. With intense curiosity he tried to get a good look at it, but he saw nothing more.

At that moment Baron, with two chandeliers in his hands, was coming up the staircase, flooding it with light. Behind him, dragging her train and gathering it up, ran Armande. She pulled a little plump-cheeked girl after her by the hand, and whispered to her:

"It's all right, it's all right, don't be afraid, Esprit, we're going to see Father!"

The nasal, sorrowful chanting of a nun could be heard from upstairs. Armande and Baron ran in and saw the nun with hands folded in prayer.

"Saint Clare . . ." thought Armande, and saw that the

[238]

whole bed and Molière himself were covered with blood. The girl was frightened and began to cry.

"Molière!" Armande said in a shaken voice, as she had never spoken to him before. But she received no answer.

And Baron quickly set the chandeliers on the table and rushed down the stairs, skipping over every second step. Clutching the servant by the lapels, he growled:

"Where did you disappear? Where's the doctor, idiot?"

And the servant answered desperately:

"Monsieur Baron, what could I do? None of them would come to Monsieur de Molière! Not one of them!"

Chapter 33
Dust Thou Art

The whole house was in a state of agonized perplexity, which communicated itself to the mendicant nuns as well. Having prayed for a time over the washed and covered Molière on his deathbed, they did not know what to do next. The point is that the earth refused to receive Monsieur Molière's body.

Jean Aubry had vainly pleaded with the priests of the Saint Eustache parish to visit the dying man. Both of them flatly refused to come. A third, taking pity on the desperate Aubry, came to the comedian's home, but it was too late. Molière was dead, and the priest hastened away. Burying Molière with the appropriate Church rites was out of the question. The sinful comedian died without a last confession and without repudiating his profession, which was condemned by the Church. Nor had he made a written promise never again to play on the stage in the event that the Lord, in his infinite mercy, restored him to health.

This formula had not been signed, and no priest in Paris

would undertake to escort Monsieur de Molière to the cemetery. Besides, no cemetery would accept him.

Armande was in despair when the Auteuil curé, François Loyseau, who had become friendly with Molière during the latter's stay in his parish, came to her aid. He not only helped her to compose a petition to the Archbishop of Paris, but, at the unquestionable risk of the gravest consequences for himself, accompanied Armande on a visit to the Archbishop.

After a few moments in the quiet waiting room, the widow and the priest were ushered into the Archbishop's study, and Armande found herself in the presence of Harlay de Champvallon, the Archbishop of Paris.

"Your Grace, I have come to beg your permission," said the widow, "to give my late husband a proper Christian burial."

De Champvallon read the petition and said to the widow, while his eyes were fixed in a heavy and intent stare on Loyseau:

"Your husband, Madame, was a comedian?"

"Yes," Armande replied with anxiety. "But he died like a good Christian. This will be attested by two nuns of the convent of Saint Clare d'Annecy, who were at our home at the time. Besides, he went to confession and communion last Easter."

"I am extremely sorry," answered the Archbishop, "but there is nothing that can be done. I cannot grant you permission for the burial."

"But what shall I do with his body?" Armande asked, crying.

[241]

"I pity him," repeated the Archbishop, "but you must understand, Madame, I cannot disrespect the law."

And Loyseau, followed by the Archbishop's heavy stare, escorted the sobbing Armande from the room.

"This means," Armande cried, hiding her face on the curé's shoulder, "that I will have to take him out of town and bury him somewhere by the roadside. . . ."

But the faithful curé did not abandon her, and they proceeded to the royal château in Saint-Germain. Here Armande had more success. The King received her. She was ushered into a room where he awaited her, standing by the table. Armande said nothing, but dropped to her knees and burst into tears. The King helped her up and asked:

"Please calm down, Madame. What can I do for you?"

"Your Majesty," said Armande, "I am not permitted to bury my husband, Molière! Please intercede for me, Your Majesty!"

The King replied:

"Everything will be done for your late husband. Go home, I beg you, and take care of the body."

Sobbing and thanking him, Armande left, and a few moments later the King's messenger rode off for de Champvallon. When the latter appeared at the château, the King asked him:

"What's all this about Molière's death?"

"Sire," replied de Champvallon. "The law forbids his burial in consecrated ground."

"And how deep is the consecrated ground?" the King asked.

"Four feet, Your Majesty," replied the Archbishop.

"Be kind enough, Archbishop, to bury him five feet deep,"

said Louis. "But be sure to bury him, avoiding either pomp or scandal."

A paper was signed in the Archbishop's office.

"In view of the circumstances uncovered in the inquiry conducted at our command, we permit the curé of the Saint Eustache parish to inter the body of the late Molière in accordance with Church ritual, on condition, however, that this interment take place without any solemnities, attended by not more than two priests; that it must not take place during the day; and that no solemn service be held for him either at the Church of Saint Eustache or at any other."

As soon as the news spread among the Paris upholsterers that the son of the late esteemed Jean-Baptiste Poquelin, the comedian de Molière, who bore the hereditary title of upholsterer, had died, representatives of the corporation appeared on the rue de Richelieu and covered the body of the comedian with the corporation's embroidered banner, thus returning Molière to the status he had voluntarily abandoned: an upholsterer he was, and to the upholsterers he returned.

At the same time, a certain ambitious man who knew that the great Condé had always been well disposed toward Molière came to Condé with the following words:

"Your Highness, allow me to submit an epitaph which I have written for Molière."

Condé took the epitaph and, glancing at the author, replied:

"Thank you. But I would have preferred it if he had written your epitaph."

On February 21, at nine in the evening, when Molière's body was to be brought out, a crowd of some hundred and fifty persons gathered at the home of the late comedian, and it is not known of whom this crowd consisted. But for some reason it conducted itself noisily; there were shouts, and even whistles. The widow of Monsieur de Molière became greatly agitated at the sight of the strangers. On the advice of her friends, she opened the window and addressed the assembly with the following words:

"Gentlemen! Why do you wish to trouble the peace of my late husband? I can assure you, he was a good man and he died like a Christian. Perhaps you will do us the honor of escorting him to the cemetery?"

Someone placed a leather purse in her hand, and she began to distribute the money. After some excitement over the money, everything quieted down, and torches appeared near the house. At nine o'clock a wooden coffin was carried out. It was preceded by two silent priests. Next to the coffin walked boys dressed in albs, carrying huge wax candles. A whole forest of flames flowed after the grave, and famous men were seen among those escorting the coffin: the painter Pierre Mignard, the fabulist La Fontaine, the poets Boileau and Chapelle. They all carried torches, and were followed by the actors of the Palais Royal troupe with torches in their hands, and by a crowd which had now grown to about two hundred. As they passed a certain street, a window opened and a woman asked in a loud voice:

"Whose funeral is this?"

"Who knows?" answered another woman. "A certain Molière's."

This Molière was brought to the cemetery of Saint Joseph and buried in the section reserved for suicides and unbaptized children. And in the Church of Saint Eustache, the priest noted briefly that on Tuesday, February 21, 1673, the upholsterer and Royal Valet Jean-Baptiste Poquelin was buried in the Saint Joseph cemetery.

Epilogue

We Bid Farewell to
the Bronze Comedian

His wife had a stone slab laid on his grave and ordered a hundred bundles of firewood delivered to the cemetery so that the homeless beggars could warm themselves. The next winter, which was especially severe, a huge fire was lit on the stone. The slab cracked from the heat and fell apart. Time scattered the pieces. And when, during the Great Revolution, one hundred and nineteen years later, the people's *commissaires* came to disinter the body of Jean-Baptiste Molière and transfer it to a mausoleum, no one could point precisely to the place of his burial. And although someone's remains were disinterred and placed in a mausoleum, no one can say with assurance that those were Molière's. It may well be that the honors were conferred on the ashes of an unknown man.

And so, my hero passed into the earth of Paris and vanished in it. And so, in the course of time, did all his manuscripts and letters, as though conjured away into thin air. It was said that the manuscripts perished in a fire, and that his letters, carefully collected by some fanatic, were then consigned by him to flames. In short, everything was lost, with the exception of two slips of paper on which the itinerant comedian had once acknowledged the receipt of certain sums of money for his troupe.

But one day, though robbed of both his manuscripts and letters, he left the plot of earth he had shared with suicides and stillborn infants and took up his place over the basin of a dried-out fountain. There he is! It is he, the King's comedian, with bronze bows on his shoes. And I, who am never to see him, send him my farewell greetings.

Moscow, 1932–1933

PLAYS BY MOLIÈRE MENTIONED IN THE TEXT

1653	*The Bungler*	*L'Étourdi*
1656	*The Amorous Quarrel*	*Le Dépit amoureux*
1658	*The Amorous Doctor*	*Le Médecin amoureux*
1659	*The Precious Ladies Ridiculed*	*Les Précieuses ridicules*
1660	*Sganarelle, or the Imaginary Cuckold*	*Sganarelle, ou le Cocu imaginaire*
1661	*Don Garcia of Navarre, or the Jealous Prince*	*Dom Garcie de Navarre, ou le Prince jaloux*
1661	*The School for Husbands*	*L'École des maris*
1661	*The Bores*	*Les Fâcheux*
1662	*The School for Wives*	*L'École des femmes*
1663	*The Critique of The School for Wives*	*La Critique de l'École des femmes*
1663	*The Versailles Impromptu*	*L'Impromptu de Versailles*
1664	*The Forced Marriage*	*Le Mariage forcé*
1664	*The Princess of Elis*	*La Princesse d'Élide*
1664	*Tartuffe (The Impostor)*	*Tartuffe (L'Imposteur)*
1665	*Don Juan, or the Stone Feast*	*Dom Juan, ou le Festin de pierre*
1665	*Love, the Doctor*	*L'Amour médecin*
1666	*The Misanthrope*	*Le Misanthrope*
1666	*The Doctor in Spite of Himself*	*Le Médecin malgré lui*
1666	*Mélicerte*	*Mélicerte*

[249]

LIST OF PLAYS

1666	*Corydon*	*Corydon*
1667	*The Sicilian, or Love the Painter*	*Le Sicilien, ou l'Amour peintre*
1668	*Amphitryon*	*Amphitryon*
1668	*George Dandin, or the Baffled Husband*	*Georges Dandin, ou le Mari confondu*
1668	*The Miser*	*L'Avare*
1669	*Monsieur de Pourceaugnac*	*Monsieur de Pourceaugnac*
1670	*The Magnificent Lovers*	*Les Amants magnifiques*
1670	*The Would-Be Gentleman*	*Le Bourgeois gentilhomme*
1671	*Psyche* (with Corneille and Quinault)	*Psyché*
1671	*The Swindles of Scapin*	*Les Fourberies de Scapin*
1671	*The Seductive Countess*	*La Comtesse d'Escarbagnas*
1672	*The Learned Ladies*	*Les Femmes savantes*
1673	*The Imaginary Invalid*	*Le Malade imaginaire*

OTHER FRENCH PLAYS MENTIONED IN THE TEXT

EDME BOURSAULT

1663	*The Portrait of a Painter, or the Counter-Critique of The School for Wives*	*Le Portrait du peintre, ou la Contre-critique de l'École des femmes*

CLAUDE BOYER

1662	*Tonaxere*	Originally called *Oropaste, ou le Faux Tonaxere*

CYRANO DE BERGERAC

1645–1649	*The Tricked Pedant*	*Le Pédant joué*

PIERRE CORNEILLE

1631	*The Widow*	*La Veuve*
1632	*The Palace Gallery*	*La Galerie du palais*
1633	*Place Royale*	*La Place Royale*
1637	*The Cid*	*Le Cid*
1640	*Cinna*	*Cinna*

List of Plays

1643	*The Death of Pompey*	*La Mort de Pompée*
1644	*Rodogune*	*Rodogune*
1646	*Heraclius*	*Héraclius*
1650	*Andromède*	*Andromède*
1651	*Nicomède*	*Nicomède*
1662	*Sertorius*	*Sertorius*
1667	*Attila*	*Attila*
1670	*Titus and Berenice*	*Tite et Bérénice*
1671	*Psyche* (with Corneille and Quinault)	*Psyché*

NICOLAS DESFONTAINES

1642	*Perside, or the Suite of the Illustrious Basset*	*Perside, ou la Suitte d'Ibrahim Bassa*
1643	*Saint Alexis, or the Dazzling Olympia*	*L'Illustre Olympie, ou Le Saint Alexis*
1644	*The Brilliant Comedian, or the Martyrdom of Saint Genet*	*L'Illustre comédien, ou le Martyre de Saint Genest*

MADEMOISELLE DES JARDINS

1665	*The Coquette*	Originally called *La Coquette, ou le Favory*

TRISTAN L'HERMITE

1645	*The Family Misfortunes of Constantine the Great*	*La Mort de Crispe*

JEAN MAGNON

1644	*Artaxerce*	*Artaxerce*
1645	*Jehosophat*	*Jehosophat*

ANTOINE-JACOB MONTFLEURY

1663	*The Hôtel de Condé Impromptu*	*L'Impromptu de l'Hôtel de Condé*

JEAN RACINE

1664	*The Theban Brothers*	*La Thebaïde, ou Les Frères ennemis*

LIST OF PLAYS

1665	*Alexander the Great* (also called *Alexander and Porus*)	*Alexandre le Grand* (*Alexandre et Porus*)
1667	*Andromaque*	*Andromaque*
1669	*Britannicus*	*Britannicus*

CARDINAL RICHELIEU WITH JEAN DESMARETZ DE SAINT-SORLIN

1641	*Mirame*	*Mirame*

DONNEAU DE VISÉ

1663	*The Marquises' Vengeance*	*Vengeance des marquis*
1663	*Zélinde, or The True Critique of The School for Wives, and a Critique of the Critique*	*Zélinde, ou la Véritable critique de l'École des femmes et la Critique de la critique*
1665	*The Coquettish Mother*	*La Mère coquette, ou les Amants brouillés*
1667	*The Fashionable Widow*	*La Veuve à la mode*

Index

INDEX

NOTE: *many names containing* de *will be found under that part of the name following* de

Index

INDEX

Index

INDEX

Index

MIKHAIL BULGAKOV, playwright, novelist, and short story writer was born in Kiev in 1891. He was graduated from medical school, practiced medicine for a short while, and then abandoned it for writing. Choosing to remain in Russia after the Revolution, Bulgakov continually had difficulty with censorship and by 1930 was barred from publication or production. *The Life of Monsieur de Molière,* completed in 1933, was not published until 1962, twenty-two years after Bulgakov's death. His monumental novel *The Master and Margarita* appeared in this country in 1967 and was hailed as a masterpiece. Other works available here are *Heart of a Dog, The Fatal Eggs,* and the plays *Flight* and *Bliss.*

MIRRA GINSBURG, born in Russia, translated *The Fatal Eggs and Other Soviet Satire,* in which the title story is by Bulgakov, *The Master and Margarita,* as well as Bulgakov's plays *Flight* and *Bliss.* Her translations of works by Isaac Babel, Isaac Bashevis Singer, and others have appeared in anthologies and such magazines as *Kenyon Review, The New Yorker,* and *Commentary.*